LORRAINE EDWARDS

DEVOTIONAL & JOURNAL

Pray It

FORWARD!

FOR WOMEN WHO CHOOSE
TO FIGHT ON THEIR KNEES

DEVOTIONAL & JOURNAL

Pray It

FORWARD!

FOR WOMEN WHO CHOOSE
TO FIGHT ON THEIR KNEES

The People

THANK YOU TO MY **Lord and Savior Jesus Christ**, who is the Word and then gave me these words to impact individuals, couples, and families now, and more importantly, for eternity.

Ebony Wilkins, you said, "Are you going to make this a book?" when I was writing daily devotional thoughts for our prayer and fasting journey. Now it is done. Thank you for being the spark that started the fire.

I was chatting with a published author friend, sharing insights, and she said, "When are you going to write your book?" This planted a seed of belief that if she did it and she thinks I can, then I probably can. **Jennifer Patterson**, thank you for planting the seed.

Andrea Lende, thank you for your genuine spirit, relentless encouragement, late-night editing, and inspiration to dream bigger for my future as an author than I would have imagined.

Ruth Hovsepian thank you for allowing me to divest myself of one part of this process by doing the design and formatting of the book. I am more grateful than you will ever know.

Thank you, **April Kidwell**, for the fast-track editing to release the book in time for the new year and for making me a better writer.

Thank you to my Beatitudes Self-Publishing cohort for cheering me on and keeping me accountable to the community.

The Inspiration

To my mother, **Irma** Edwards, and sister, **Heather Akpan**. Thank you for giving me the runway to make this crazy dream fly.

To **Tracey** and **Rene**. Thank you for being friends who cheer, encourage, and uplift me. Your support and belief kept me going when I was ready to give up.

To the extraordinary women who choose to fast and pray for the conversion, healing, wholeness, and spiritual growth of the beloved men in their lives, church, and community, I dedicate this devotional to you.

As you embark on this journey of spiritual connection and growth, may this resource serve as a guiding light, providing you with inspiration and a sacred space to pour your heart out to your Heavenly Father.

May your prayers be a source of strength, healing, and transformation, not only for this beloved man in your life but also for your soul.

In the quiet moments of reflection and intercession, may you find the peace and guidance you seek, and may your prayers bring blessings and harmony to him and the world around you.

With heartfelt gratitude for allowing me to be a part of your journey,

Contents

Foreword

THERE EXISTS FOR BELIEVERS a profound and often underestimated power — the power of prayer. It is a force that transcends boundaries, connects hearts, and brings solace to the soul.

Pray It Forward will help women harness the power to intercede for the men in their lives. Lorraine invites us to embark on a sacred journey where the gentle whispers of women's prayers around the world converge to offer hope, healing, and empowerment for the men in our lives.

Although we know the power of prayer, being obedient to God's call for us to stand in the gap for others can be difficult...particularly when we are unsure of the outcome. This has often been my experience. Lorraine has been one of my best friends for well over 20 years. During some of the most difficult times in my life, her encouragement, and sometimes admonition, has consistently been to pray. Pray for my children, pray for my marriage, and most importantly, pray for my husband. Especially when I didn't want to pray. But I trust her, and I trust her relationship with God, so I prayed. I agonized. I doubted. I believed. I tried to back out. But in the end, I was closer to God for my obedience. Regardless of what your flesh tells you, this is a divine process. Trust it.

We are in a spiritual battle that is as impactful as what we are seeing in the world today. We are in a war against the enemy of our souls for the physical and eternal lives of our men. Our brothers, our sons, our cousins, our husbands, our friends. They need the uniquely powerful prayers of the women who love them. They need our sacrifice of comfort and time to petition God on their behalf. It's not easy, but it's worth it.

Pray It Forward taps into the strength residing within every woman's heart, a strength finding expression not only in words but also in our consistent communion with God. The discipline of intentional prayer for thirty-one days will benefit those of us who are praying, as much as it will benefit those we are praying for. Through poignant anecdotes, heartfelt reflections, and a wealth of wisdom, Lorraine, encourages us to embrace the sacred duty of prayer, offering it as a gift to the men who grace our lives.

As we turn the pages, may we discover the beauty of vulnerability, the strength in surrender, and the boundless grace that emerges when women unite in prayer. In this act of devotion, we become conduits of love, peace, and resilience, that have the power to uplift, transform, and heal.

May this book serve as a guide, an inspiration, and a source of comfort for all who embark on this sacred journey of prayer. May the words within these pages resonate in the hearts of women, nurturing a community of prayerful souls dedicated to uplifting the men in their lives.

Ebony Wilkins

How Does Prayer "Work"?

PRAYER. WHAT FEELINGS DOES this word engender for you? Peace, anxiety, joy, insecurity, hope, or unworthiness? For me, it was always a bit of all of those. And to be honest, it still feels that way sometimes.

If you had asked me what my first book would be, prayer would not have been in the top 20 list of topics.

In the vast tapestry of human existence, there exists a thread woven by the hands of the faithful, a thread known as prayer. It is a thread that, for many, remains an enigma — a mysterious connection to the divine, often left unexplored and misunderstood.

Prayer is the quintessential answer to every problem believers can't solve on their own. It is the panacea for all ills for which the pastor has no answer. It is the crutch that supports our shaky faith amid crises.

But what is it really? What is the point of it? How do you do it? Is there a right way?

For years, I also grappled with the perplexing nature of prayer, wrestling with questions that seemed to elude me at every turn. Why did it seem as if my prayers went unanswered? Was there truly a purpose to my petitions, or were they merely whispers into the void?

These are all thoughts and questions I had throughout my lifetime in church as a believer. I didn't verbalize them, of course. That would have been totally unacceptable, akin to heresy, probably. But true, nevertheless.

I just didn't get it.

Honestly, sometimes it seemed because I didn't understand prayer and all its assumed intricacies, I also didn't benefit from it.

I prayed many prayers I felt went unanswered (I guess the answer was "no.") Good prayers. Legitimate, God-honoring prayers seemed to hit the ceiling and fall back to the floor.

I, like YOU, struggled to find connection and power in my prayers. It was a struggle that persisted for much of my life, leaving me with a sense of futility, frustration, and faithlessness.

My prayers felt like one-sided conversations, a monologue into the abyss, with no discernible response from the heavens.

And in those times, it just left me more confused about how this prayer thing "worked."

I believed God was good! I had even heard of other people's prayers being answered in the affirmative and even the miraculous, which both emboldened *and* confused me.

Everything in the Bible says God loves us all equally. If He did miraculous and amazing things for others, He would do it for me too. Right?

On the other hand, I hadn't witnessed those types of prayers in my life.

Maybe I was just doing it wrong.

Maybe I didn't have enough faith.

Maybe I had unforgiven sin in my heart.

Maybe I wasn't praying in His will.

Maybe, maybe, maybe...

This litany of "maybes" distanced me spiritually and emotionally from God as it related to prayer.

I was always active in church, service, evangelism, and ministry, but prayer was my spiritual Achilles' heel.

You are probably saying, "It sounds like you are the last person who should be writing a devotional on intercessory prayer."

Yep. It sure does. And I am.

But God...

In 2005, I read the book referenced as the motivation for this devotional, *Steps to Christ*. It was a book I had read several times before. But I experienced it differently this time. It enamored me with a beautiful and profoundly engaging picture of Christ and His love for us I had seen, but not personalized before this time.

Suddenly, prayer became a constant and open conversation between the lover of my soul and me.

We all know when we are in love with a guy, all we want to do is talk to him, hang out with him, and share with him.

This became my posture with Christ. Prayer became the medium by which that was possible.

Then my prayers also shifted. God started waking me up at 2 or 3 a.m. to pray. Not for myself anymore, but for others.

The list kept getting longer and longer until I would often be awake praying for up to 2 hours, interceding for the marriages, lives, loneliness, sickness, and salvation of others.

In 2019, when my friend's marriage was in shambles, and she was ready to quit after many years of unhappiness and unfulfillment, I said, "Let's pray." We had prayed many times before, but never like this.

I told her I had just listened to a message the previous day about how men are under attack by the enemy because if he can get them, he can destroy families, churches, communities, and ultimately, society.

I asked her to commit to 30 days of prayer and fasting for her husband, not her marriage, not her family, not for her happiness, just for him. I said I would write a short devotional for each day and some things to pray for. She reluctantly agreed.

Thirty days later, the foundation of this devotional, *Pray It Forward: For Women Who Choose to Fight on Their Knees*, was created.

And we prayed for every theme and prayer point in this journal. And you know what happened?

Was their marriage transformed, her husband give his life fully to Christ, and the family live happily ever after?

Unfortunately, no. None of that.

Honestly, I had some questions for God after that intercessory time. Where was our miracle?

But do you want to know what DID happen?

My friend was transformed.

She connected with God differently.

She engaged with the lover of her soul deeply.

She took divorce off the table forever.

She recommitted to the covenant she had made.

She began showing up differently in her marriage.

And because of all those changes in her, they are still together today, and their marriage is better than ever.

God showed me some miracles happen immediately; some over time. And sometimes, He answers the prayer we didn't know we needed to pray.

This devotional is not a promise of miraculous transformation in the one God has assigned to you for this time, although I believe with my whole heart, God can do that.

Nothing you can see may change about him immediately. God wants him more than you do, so we know He is always working.

But everything can change about you.

Welcome to *Pray It Forward*, where we will believe and activate the transformative power of intercessory prayer and embark on a journey of faith, hope, and connection that will leave a lasting impact not only on our lives but also on the lives of the ones for whom we are praying.

Fasting

S TILL WET FROM THE waters of the Jordan, glowing from the light of Heaven's glory upon Him, heart full of the words of approval of His Father, Jesus was driven into the wilderness by the Spirit to be tempted by the devil. There, He fasted 40 days and 40 nights, preparing Himself for the test Satan would bring to bear in the battle for the redemption of man.

There is a well-known story in the gospels about a father who brought his son to the disciples because a demon possessed him. Nine disciples were there waiting for Jesus, Peter, James, and John to come down from the Mount of Transfiguration. But none of the nine remaining disciples could heal the boy and expel the demon.

When Jesus came down and saw the scene, the man brought his son to Jesus, telling Him of the disciples' failure, and Jesus rebuked the demon, and saved the boy.

In private, the ashamed disciples ask why they had failed. Remember, they had been evangelizing, healing, and casting out demons all over the Jewish region. Now, they failed.

Matthew 17:20, 21 — So Jesus said to them, "Because of your unbelief; for assuredly, I say to you, if you have faith as a mustard seed, you will say to this mountain, 'Move from here to there' and it will move, and nothing will be impossible for you. However, this kind does not go out except by prayer ***and fasting***."

Throughout scripture and spiritual history, believers have employed fasting with prayer to address their most pressing strongholds and crises. Not as a ritual to impress God, but as a sacrifice and a tool expressing complete surrender and dependence on God for physical sustenance and spiritual victory.

Esther, David, Daniel, Paul, Jesus, and many others in the Bible prayed and fasted to gain victory, clarity, and power in crisis.

The fact you have picked up this book indicates you are in your moment of crisis and willing to surrender the physical to connect on a deeper level with the power of the Spirit.

True fasting is to refrain from food in its entirety for a designated period. We always encourage drinking water throughout food fasts.

I **DO NOT recommend refraining from food during the thirty-one days of this intercession unless you have been so instructed by God and have consulted with your physician.

However, I believe for this to be most effective, there needs to be a sacrifice of the flesh which is then substituted with prayer throughout the day.

I have included some suggestions you can select based on your capacity:

1. Fast from food completely for twenty-four hours or one day each of the four weeks of the thirty-one-day intercession. I recommend picking one day of the week and being consistent. Please drink water throughout the day.

2. Eat two meals a day and fast and pray during the third meal for the entire intercession, i.e., eat breakfast and lunch, but fast and pray through dinner.

3. If you have health conditions that prevent you from skipping meals, a great option is removing all processed food from your meals for thir-

ty-one days. Eliminate anything in a box, bag, or can. Then, designate the time before or after eating each meal to pray for the theme of the day.

4. Eliminate all drinks except water during this time. I strongly encourage you to eliminate alcohol, so you are clear in your mind and able to hear and follow the Holy Spirit's leadership.

5. In addition to any food-related fasting, you can also eliminate social media, television, or gaming for the month and pray when you typically scroll, watch, or play.

These are just some suggestions that align with the spiritual ideas of fasting. Sacrifice what pleases the flesh to focus on what pleases the Spirit.

I strongly recommend praying about what the fast will be for you. **Do not leave this part out**. I believe you have engaged with this book because you have a significant burden for the one God has entrusted to your intercession.

Do not allow the flesh to win and him to lose.

Remember that when you surrender to the Lord, He will always work for your good and His glory.

Psalm 37:5 (NKJV) — "Commit your way to the Lord, trust also in Him, and He shall bring it to pass."

If the Spirit drove our Savior and Lord to fast and pray in preparation for His encounter with the enemy and fulfillment of the plan of redemption, how much more critical is it for us as sinful humans to do the same as we fight for the salvation of those we love?

God bless you on your journey.

Disclaimer

INFORMATION PROVIDED IN THIS book is intended for general informational purposes only and should not be considered medical advice. The author is not a medical professional, and the content herein should not be used as a substitute for professional medical advice, diagnosis, or treatment.

Fasting, like any dietary or lifestyle change, may have varying effects on individuals depending on their unique medical conditions, health status, and personal circumstances. The author of this book cannot and does not assume any responsibility for any negative consequences or adverse effects that may arise from implementing fasting or related practices suggested in this book.

Readers must recognize fasting can impact one's health and well-being, and any decision to engage in fasting should be made with careful consideration of individual medical capacity. Before starting any fasting regimen or changing one's diet or lifestyle, readers are strongly encouraged to consult with a qualified healthcare professional, such as a physician or registered dietitian, to assess their medical suitability for fasting and to receive personalized guidance tailored to their specific needs.

Readers should also know fasting may carry risks, and these risks may be elevated for individuals with certain medical conditions, such as diabetes, heart disease, or eating disorders. Therefore, it is of utmost importance to seek professional medical advice before embarking on any fasting program.

By reading and using the information provided in this book, readers acknowledge and accept full responsibility for their decisions regarding fasting and its potential impact on their health. The author disclaims any liability for any outcomes resulting from the reader's fasting practices and strongly encourages all readers to prioritize their health and well-being by seeking professional medical guidance and support.

The Discipline of Praise

Y OU KNOW BY NOW prayer was not natural for me even as a Christian until I nurtured my relationship with God differently.

Praise is similar. And to be honest, I still struggle in this area. Disentangling praise from thanksgiving is tricky because they are connected. This happens often in Christian circles.

We want to praise, but we end up thanking God.

Now, to be clear, thanksgiving to God is a great thing, a critical thing. And during these next thirty-one days, you should do both.

But it is not the same as praise.

So, you may ask, "What is the difference, and why does it matter?"

Praise is honoring God for who He is, and thanksgiving is honoring him for what He has done.

The main reason it matters, especially in the context of fasting and prayer for your beloved, is God's work may not be obvious during the thirty-one days or for weeks, months, or even years after this intercession is "over." It would be easy to neglect honoring God for what He has done if you think He has done nothing because you see nothing.

If after thirty-one days of intercession, the relationship you are praying for remains a wreck, you may think you have nothing for which to thank God.

But when you praise Him because of who He is: Lord, Savior, faithful Father, lover of your soul, Jehovah-Jireh; you will recognize He is still worthy of praise after the intercessory period no matter what you see happening.

Because of that, the second half of this journal is thirty-one days of praise.

After spending thirty-one days fasting and praying, commit to following up with thirty-one days of praising.

Psalm 22:3 says in the King James Version, "But thou art holy, O thou that inhabitest the praises of Israel."

Other than saying "inhabitest" with a 21st-century tongue being challenging, this is an amazing declaration of how God interacts with our praise.

The word inhabitest is *yâshab* in the Hebrew and it means to sit down, to dwell, to remain, to settle, to marry, and many other similar terms.

God is busy running the universe, and yet He sits down and dwells with us in our praise.

What better leverage can you have on your beloved's heart than to have God dwelling in you?

Every time you praise God–it is not just a conversation between you and Him–it is an invitation to your Abba to stay.

Imagine every time you praise, God is sitting on the couch, or in your office, or at the gym working on the heart of the one entrusted to you, softening it, molding it, nurturing him to be the husband, son, father, employer, boyfriend, or neighbor He created him to be.

Psalm 34:1 NKJV says, "I will bless the Lord at all times; His praise shall continually be in my mouth."

If you praise Him continually, you have invited God to move in and not just spend time.

And let's not forget while praise is changing him, it is changing you, too.

Praise reminds you even if you don't see a miraculous transformation at the end of the thirty-one days of prayer, God has never stopped working for the heart of your beloved and the strength of your relationship with him.

Thanksgiving will be a part of this. But we have included scriptures you can repeat to help you praise when you struggle to be thankful. Besides scripture, I have included thirty-one of my favorite praise and worship songs for each day that you can play to help you keep your focus during the day. We will include a list of all the songs in the index for your reference. You may even want to utilize this playlist during challenging times apart from this study. He is worthy.

You can trust Him.

So let's praise the Lord.

Your Divine Assignment

Y OU PICKED UP THIS book because there is a man in your life whom God has put on your heart to intercede for.

This man is your divine assignment. Originally this was a devotional for wives praying for their husbands, a very clear and direct target. The Holy Spirit impressed me to develop this book further to include fathers, sons, brothers, or even future husbands.

Essentially, any woman would have a guide to praying for any man in their life.

Great idea, God! I love it!

Then I had to sit down and re-write. And I was no longer excited.

Why?

I said "your husband" over 100 times in the book because I knew who I was talking to and whom I was talking about.

Now, I didn't know. I wanted it to be any and every man. But what word encapsulates any and every man with the same clarity and intimacy as "your husband"?

If you are committing sixty-two days to have this man in the forefront of your prayers and praise, he will not be a stranger on the street. You will have a connection to him, love him, and want so much for God to work in him you will sacrifice food, time, and self.

The short answer is there was initially no word that encompassed every possible scenario of why a woman would pray for a man.

I combed through the thesaurus, talked to a friend, and called on AI to help me with something warm, loving, and clear. I finally found it. And when I saw it, it made me think of the apostles because it was one of their favorite ways to address the churches in his letter.

Beloved. A much-loved person.

Like the apostles, your heart is tied to the salvation, transformation, and healing of this person.

Most of the writers of the letters in the New Testament used the word beloved to address those they were praying for, rebuking, greeting, and praising.

1 John 4:1 — Beloved, if God so loved us, we also ought to love one another.

Jude 1:17 — But you, beloved, remember the words which were spoken before by the apostles of our Lord Jesus Christ:

II Peter 3:14 — Therefore, beloved, looking forward to these things, be diligent to be found by Him in peace, without spot and blameless;

Philippians 2:12 — Therefore, my beloved, as you have always obeyed, not as in my presence only, but now much more in my absence, work out your salvation with fear and trembling.

When you think of the word beloved, the feelings generated require you to be attentive to this relationship, this person, and therefore to this commitment to intercession.

Throughout this devotional, you will see the phrase "your beloved". For our purposes, this is the man you cared enough about to surrender yourself to get a breakthrough for him. Whether that is your husband, father, son, brother, boyfriend, pastor, or co-worker, he is beloved.

You will see other phrases that refer to him, such as *your divine assignment, your loved one, the one entrusted to your intercession*, etc.

They all mean the one for whom the Holy Spirit convicted you to intercede.

And so, pray it forward, my beloved sister, for your beloved brother.

Coloring Time

A s a child, I loved to color. I didn't do any of those random scribbles that all parents are obliged to gush over and put up on the refrigerator.

No. I was serious about coloring. My nature required it to be precisely in the lines, with attention to the details and colors that complement one another. This was a thing.

It was fun and relaxing.

With the weight of intercession, fasting, praising, actively loving, and let's not forget all the other responsibilities women have that cannot be delayed for sixty-two days, I thought I would add a coloring page.

Why? Maybe you enjoyed them too when life didn't "life" so much. A time when things were a lot slower, more relaxed, and just fun.

For many, though not all, that time is called childhood. It didn't last as long as adulthood lasts, which seems incredibly unfair. Yet, in those few years, it provided designated time for coloring.

We can't go backward, but maybe we can bring some good things from the past to the present. Coloring seems like a good place to start.

When I googled coloring, it appeared I was correct as adult coloring pages are all the rage.

I added the scripture for each day to help you focus and remember that God is with you now and forever.

So even if you skip "show and tell", designate some time to relax, take your mind off everything, and color.

Navigating This Devotional & Journal

Thirty-one Days of Fasting and Prayer

In the first half of *Pray It Forward*, I have devotional thoughts and prayer points for thirty-one days on different themes that can impact the life of the one for whom you will be praying. It is not comprehensive. However, I tried to include relevant issues men face in the world today so women can bring them to the altar on behalf of the one divinely assigned to them.

Use this devotional to intercede for your husband, son, brother, father, pastor, friend, co-worker, or even your future husband.

This was initially developed for a man who is not a disciple of Christ, so there are themes of salvation and sin that may not apply to the one you are praying for if he has a relationship with God. You can skip a theme that may not seem to apply to your situation.

With that being said, I would not dismiss any issue too quickly because although, as written, it may not fit, there may be an aspect of salvation or forgiveness or marriage that applies to him, and you can insert the appropriate reflection and prayer points in your journal and intercede based on that.

Be honest and open with the Lord about your concerns for this man God has called you to pray for. Lay them at His feet, knowing "He cares for you."

Each day includes a devotional thought, an example reflection, and some specific prayer points for the day. This book also includes:

- A Journal section for your reflections about your beloved.

- A section for additional prayer requests.

- A section to reflect on how fasting and prayer are impacting you.

- A section for things God is revealing to you each day.

- A section to record praise and thanksgiving for the day.

- A fun coloring page with the scripture for each devotional.

When you spend time in intentional prayer about the way God is moving, you will see things for which to praise Him.

Don't skip these sections. Don't just think about them in your head.

Write them down daily!

There is power in taking the time to truly reflect on what God is doing, how you feel and think through this process, what you see in your beloved's life, and how God is changing you. You will be amazed when you look back in thirty-one days and read what you wrote on day five versus day twenty-five. Don't think you will remember. You won't. Write it down.

Commit to setting aside time to pray and write in the journal for these thirty-one days. I prefer the morning as my time to make sure it happens, and life doesn't interrupt me. Doing it in the morning also sets your focus for the day early. And of course, you will pray throughout the day.

However, if the morning doesn't work for you, set a time that does and commit to it.

I included example reflections to help you think more broadly and give more depth to your prayers. I struggle with surface, aimless prayers when I am not focused. These examples are to help you get focused on what exactly the concerns for your beloved are and what you want God to do in his life.

I have included scripture for each day, and there is an index in the back with all the scriptures so you can have easy access in case you forget one.

In addition, there is an index with all the themes so if you want to go back and spend another day, week, or month just on one or more specific themes, you can find them easily.

Fast from something during the thirty-one days of prayer. Recommendations about how to fast based on your medical and life circumstances are included in the "about fasting" section.

Thirty-one Days of Praise

In the second half of *Pray It Forward*, we have devotional thoughts and praise points for thirty-one days on the same themes we prayed for during the intercession.

Don't skip this part. We have already discussed the power of praise and although we have a small section in the prayer devotionals for you to give daily praise, this complete thirty-one days is a sacrifice of praise to our God.

Approach these thirty-one days in a structured way, by praising through each topic as you prayed through them for the last thirty-one days. Thank God for the things that have and/or will come to pass. Use the scriptures in the journal as a starting point for your worship. Or you can start your worship with praise with the song and allow the Holy Spirit to direct you to the day's topic, based on what He sees as a priority. Either way is effective.

Pray for God to expand your understanding of how to truly praise Him. Ask the Holy Spirit to make your praise pure and sweet to our God's nostrils. Think about the goodness of God and the promises He has given us in His Word. Think of how the scripture writers expressed their love and awe for our Creator God. The Alpha and Omega. The Beginning and the End. The Author and Finisher of our faith!

The next thirty-one days will draw you so much closer to God and will change your perspective on how you see life.

To help you navigate this and keep focused on your praise, I have included:

- Journal section for writing your praise.

- Journal section for thanksgiving.

- A praise and worship song for the day.

- A coloring page with the scripture for each day.

We have all purchased books, journals, and devotionals we started and never finished. I am not immune.

But you can do anything for sixty-two days. And since I believe this man is divinely assigned to you for this intercession, he is your "why." I believe it is a big enough "why" to prevent even the enemy from getting you off course.

I have been praying for you since I wrote the introduction. And I continue.

God bless you on this journey of a lifetime.

The Motivation

"Our Heavenly Father waits to bestow upon us the fullness of His blessing. It is our privilege to drink largely at the fountain of boundless love. What a wonder it is that we pray so little. God is ready and willing to hear the sincere prayer of the humblest of His children.

Why should the sons and daughters of God be reluctant to pray, when prayer is the key in the hand of faith to unlock heaven's storehouse where are treasured the boundless resources of omnipotence?"

Steps to Christ, p.94

Pray It

FORWARD!

Day 1

CASTING ASIDE THE DARKNESS

Genesis 1:3 — Then God said, "Let there be light, and there was light."

V ERY FEW PEOPLE LIKE the darkness. Something is unsettling and foreboding about being in the dark. Even though we all know our homes like the back of our hands, we still turn on the light as soon as we walk in the door. Why? When we walk in the dark, we can't see where we are, where we're going, or what may be in the way of our path.

If I am in an unfamiliar place, the darkness can be scary and make things look out of proportion or seem to be something they are not. In the dark, objects are hardly ever what they appear to be.

Secrets and deception live in the dark.

But Jesus is the Light! John 1:9 declares Jesus brings light to every man who comes into this world. This verse includes the best person, the worst person, and everyone in between. He brings clarity so we can see things as they are, not what the darkness makes them seem to be. His light brings freedom, clarity, and truth, and it is marvelous. When God created the light, he later filled the earth with beauty that was non-existent prior.

No life can survive where there is no light.

Write a personal reflection about your beloved so you can be specific when you intercede on his behalf. You can take pieces of the example as appropriate and add different aspects that apply to him.

(**Example**) He lives in darkness. He dwells in it. It follows him around like a cloud and encloses him like a blanket. In that state, everything is scary. Vulnerability, surrender, intimacy, love, humility; all are scary because those are unfamiliar places.

They weren't places where anyone took him as a child and showed him that he could be safe with the right people. And maybe, even as an adult, any attempts to try those places have reinforced them as unsafe. So now they are foreign and scary. But he longs for light. He reads the Bible daily because he desires to escape the darkness.

At present, his mind possesses knowledge, but his heart lacks enlightenment.

Reflection on your beloved:

_____

_____

_____

Today, as we begin this 31-day intercessory journey with God, let us pray (as applicable) that:

- God will speak the words, "Let there be light" into your beloved's heart.

- God will take all the scriptures in his head and give him an experience with them in his heart.

- God will take away the darkness in and around him and make something bright and beautiful.

- He will recognize and acknowledge only God could have brought light into his path.

- In the light of God's love, he will no longer see vulnerability, surrender, intimacy, love, and humility as scary, but as safe.

Add any additional prayer requests for him.

_____

_____

_____

Reflection on your prayer and fasting time:

_____

_____

_____

God's revelation to you today:

_____

_____

_____

Praise and Thanksgiving:

_____

_____

_____

Then God said,

Let there be light...
Genesis 1:3

Day 2

FILLING THE GOD-SIZED VOID

Jeremiah 31:3 — The Lord has appeared of old to me, saying: "Yes, I have loved you with an everlasting love; therefore with lovingkindness I have drawn you."

I LOVE JIGSAW PUZZLES. The harder it is, the more pieces it has, the more enjoyable it is for me. Because I enjoy it so much and have spent so much time doing it, I can discern the slightest difference between a piece and the space that I am trying to fill. It is not uncommon for me to look through the pieces and pick up the right one just from examination.

Occasionally, however, there are pieces, colors, and designs that are so close to the right piece I put them in the wrong space. Though a small part of me is unsure, I leave it because it seems so right. And until I find the right piece, I believe this is the right one.

We were all created with a God-sized space in our hearts and only He is the right fit. When Adam walked in perfection upon the earth, it was God who showed him that he needed a helper fit for him. But Adam's first love was God. The breath he breathed was God's. The first face he saw was God's. The first look of love he received came from God.

And even after God gave him a wife, God still held the first place in Adam's heart...at first.

Then came sin. How? In the garden, when Adam knew Eve ate the fruit and he willingly, knowingly followed her into sin, Adam moved God from His rightful place as first in his life and made Eve his new god. According to the Bible, Eve was deceived, Adam was not. He chose Eve and her fate over God and His command.

Godless men have had a God-sized void in their hearts ever since.

Write a personal reflection about your beloved so you can be specific when you intercede on his behalf. You can take pieces of the example as appropriate and add different aspects that apply to him.

(Example) He has lived his life with a God-sized void in his heart that he has tried to fill with many things, including Biblical knowledge. And yet the emptiness remains. Why? Because no one and nothing can ever fill the place where God is supposed to be. Information about God cannot fill His emptiness.

Only a relationship with God can fill that void.

Reflection on your beloved:

On Day 2, let us pray (as applicable) that:

1. Your beloved will recognize his emptiness has nothing to do with anyone or anything external, not doing or being what he wants.

2. He will long for and start searching for the missing piece in his life.

3. God will make himself known in the light and show how perfectly He fits in that void.

4. God will fill him with the love He is, and the void will disappear forever.

5. He will release everyone from the responsibility of making him whole.

Add any additional prayer requests for him.

_____

_____

_____

Reflection on your prayer and fasting time:

_____

_____

_____

God's revelation to you today:

_____

_____

_____

Praise and Thanksgiving:

_____

_____

_____

I have loved you

with an everlasting love...

Jeremiah 31:3

Day 3

Discovering Joy in the Divine

Psalm 16:11 — You will show me the path of life; In Your presence is fullness of joy; At Your right hand are pleasures forevermore.

Most people use joy and happiness as synonyms. The dictionary defines them with the same words. The Bible defines joy not just as a state of feeling, but as a state of being. In Galatians 5, Paul includes it as a fruit of the Spirit. It dwells in you as the Spirit dwells in you. If the Holy Spirit leaves, so does joy. But it doesn't come and go with life's ups and downs. Those who embody this fruit cannot keep it a secret. It overflows in them.

Even in the most difficult of life situations, joy remains.

This doesn't mean there is never sadness about events in your life or family or the world. There are many things we should be sad about. Many things about human nature demand an expression of grief. We should be angry about the hate, violence, and division in this world, though we need not sin. There are many reasons to cry out to God, "How long...?"

But when we are walking with the Holy Spirit, we don't stay in those experiences of sadness, anger, or depression because we have a foundation of joy in the Lord.

Write a personal reflection about your beloved so you can be specific when you intercede on his behalf. You can take pieces of the example as appropriate and add different aspects that apply to him.

(**Example**) For most of his life, he has not been happy, let alone joyful. The weight he carries drags down his spirit. He can fake it when he needs to for business or other things, but there is a palpable sadness that lives in him every day. As he opens himself to the Light and allows God to fill Him, we know his state of being will change. We want him to experience the fullness of joy God's presence brings.

Reflection on your beloved:

>————————————————————————————————————<

>————————————————————————————————————<

>————————————————————————————————————<

>————————————————————————————————————<

On Day 3, let us pray (as applicable) that:

1. God will gift him with the fruit of joy. This one is critical to him seeing God differently.

2. He will accept the gift and not stay in his sadness because it is familiar and comfortable.

3. He will recognize and acknowledge God alone is the source of his joy, and it cannot be found in another person.

4. He will release everyone else from responsibility for his feelings.

5. He will hold on to the source of his joy even in difficult times.

6. His family and friends will see the change in him, and he will be a witness for Christ.

Add any additional prayer requests for him.

_____

_____

_____

_____

Reflection on your prayer and fasting time:

_____

_____

_____

_____

God's revelation to you today:

_____

_____

_____

_____

Praise and Thanksgiving:

_____

_____

_____

_____

In Your presence

is fullness of joy...

Psalm 16:11

Day 4

THIRSTY NO MORE

John 4:13-14 — Jesus answered and said unto her, whosoever drinketh of this water shall thirst again: But whosoever drinketh of the water that I shall give him shall never thirst; but the water that I shall give him shall be in him a well of water springing up into everlasting life.

MANY PEOPLE WHO REJECT Christianity do so for good reasons. Many Christians don't represent Christ very well at all. And even those who do good things rarely give a clear and beautiful picture of who Christ is and what a relationship with Him means. Most of the world believes Christianity is about giving up fun stuff, following a bunch of rules, and going to church on the Sabbath. This does not sound appealing, even to me, as a committed follower of Christ.

But Christ is beautiful and faithful. He is love. He keeps his relational covenant with His people and is with us through all of life's joys and sorrows. He doesn't fail. He never betrays us. He is dependable in all circumstances. A relationship with Christ means freeing us for the truly fun stuff that has no detrimental consequences. We learn to recognize those rules as a fence of protection against the enemy's traps and not a prison.

We get to commune with Him every day, not just on the Sabbath.

Write a personal reflection about your beloved so you can be specific when you intercede on his behalf. You can take pieces of the example as appropriate and add different aspects that apply to him.

(**Example**) Most relationships in his life have been dysfunctional, self-centered, inconsistent, and even tumultuous. With this background, trusting a relationship with Christ is not appealing, even with the knowledge that God differs from people. He has never seen the beauty of Christ nor understood the freedom that comes with a relationship with Him. His experience is keeping him from seeing God as love.

God is other-centered. Consistent. Forgiving. God never fails. God gives freedom.

God...Is.

Reflection on your beloved:

_____

_____

_____

On Day 4, as we intercede, let us pray (as applicable) that:

1. God will show him the beauty of His character in a personally impactful way.

2. He will recognize he is thirsty and has been for a long time, yet unsatisfied.

3. He will consider this idea of having a relationship with Jesus with an open mind and heart.

4. God will give your beloved a taste of the living water, the rest, and the

freedom found only in relationship with Him.

5. He will experience God's love.

Add any additional prayer requests for him.

_____

_____

_____

Reflection on your prayer and fasting time:

_____

_____

_____

God's revelation to you today:

_____

_____

_____

Praise and Thanksgiving:

_____

_____

_____

Whoever drinks of the water I give...

will never thirst.

John 4:14

Day 5

CULTIVATING A SPIRIT OF GRATITUDE

1 Thessalonians 5:18 — In everything give thanks; for this is the will of God in Christ Jesus for you.

GRATITUDE IS A DISCIPLINE often lacking in American culture. This was not always the case, but as we became more technologically advanced, we have become more relationally regressed. Material consumption became the norm, and wanting more and more stuff kept us hustling from dusk to dawn to bring home the bacon. Yet in the hustle, many have lost the ability to be grateful for what they have.

Even among the non-Christian influencers of our day, a "gratitude" doctrine is being revived.

The challenging part is this spirit of consumption and ingratitude has infected Christians. Our prayers reflect this. We never forget to ask God for things, but we must be reminded to give thanks with cute little acronyms about what should happen in prayer. Yet the Bible is full of scriptures instructing and imploring us to give thanks to God for who He is, not simply for what He does. He is good! Not ice cream good; good beyond our imagination.

And yet we miss the best part of the conversation with Him when we pray...giving thanks!

Write a personal reflection about your beloved so you can be specific when you intercede on his behalf. You can take pieces of the example as appropriate and add different aspects that apply to him.

(Example) He has lived many years not seeing anything to be grateful for. There have indeed been many hurdles in his path. These challenges have diminished his gratefulness. This perspective supports the darkness covering him, and the darkness supports this mindset. And so, he continues in the vicious cycle. And yet, if his mindset shifted, he would find so many things for which to be grateful.

Reflection on your beloved:

›————————————————————————————————————‹

›————————————————————————————————————‹

›————————————————————————————————————‹

›————————————————————————————————————‹

On Day 5, let us pray (as applicable) that:

1. He will shift his mindset to one of gratitude.

2. Every day, he will see at least one thing for which to be grateful.

3. God will impress him to be intentional about expressing gratitude to his family.

4. He will see glimpses of God and His goodness and give thanks for those things.

5. He will not allow the challenges in his life to blind him to the blessings in his life.

Add any additional prayer requests for him.

>———————————————————————————————<

>———————————————————————————————<

>———————————————————————————————<

>———————————————————————————————<

Reflection on your prayer and fasting time:

>———————————————————————————————<

>———————————————————————————————<

>———————————————————————————————<

>———————————————————————————————<

God's revelation to you today:

>———————————————————————————————<

>———————————————————————————————<

>———————————————————————————————<

>———————————————————————————————<

Praise and Thanksgiving:

>———————————————————————————————<

>———————————————————————————————<

>———————————————————————————————<

>———————————————————————————————<

In everything give thanks for

this is God's will.

1 Thessalonians 5 : 18

Day 6

CONVERSATIONS WITH GOD

Matthew 6:6 — But you, when you pray, go into your room, and when you have shut your door, pray to your Father who is in the secret place; and your Father who sees in secret will reward you openly.

PRAYER IS PROBABLY ONE of the most misunderstood, misused, and underused disciplines of the Christian life. Some find it boring. Others; repetitive. Some don't pray because it hasn't "worked" in the past. Many, if not most, use it as a last resort. If all else fails, let's pray about it. And even then, the prayers are lackluster and often presumptuous.

We promise to pray for people, but then forget. Why? Because we don't believe in prayer as a real "thing." If we are honest, we know this is true, or at least it has been true at some point in our lives. We believe in God, but we don't believe IN God. We believe He exists and is good, true, powerful, and provider. We just don't believe He will do those things for us.

Prayer is the key to accessing the things God has already promised us; salvation, forgiveness, mercy, comfort, release from the burdens we carry, peace, joy, light, provision, protection, and victory in all areas of life. Why do we ignore, resist, or minimize God's promise to us in our secret place? He will not only meet us there, but He will reward us openly.

Prayer should be the first and last choice in the bad times and the good times. The first prayer is to get guidance; the second is to thank Him for the victory.

We fail because we fail to pray. We succeed when we surrender in prayer. The reason? Prayer is not about outcomes, i.e. getting what you want. Prayer is about opportunity. The opportunity to snuggle up with our Heavenly DAD, let Him wrap His arms around us, and tell Him about our day, our struggles, our joys, weaknesses, strengths, failures, and victories.

Then we get to listen to Him tell us about His vision, His protection, His direction, His plans, and His love for us.

Write a personal reflection about your beloved so you can be specific when you intercede on his behalf. You can take pieces of the example as appropriate and add different aspects that apply to him.

(Example) He has been resistant to prayer in his life in a consistent way. Only God knows the reason in his heart. He, like many others, sees prayer as just a thing we do when we don't know what to do. Or he has prayed about something important, and it hasn't "worked." But whatever the reason, we know God needs to intervene. Because without prayer, there is no power.

Reflection on your beloved:

On Day 6, let us pray (as applicable) that:

1. God will speak to him so clearly about how to address a situation he is struggling with and he won't be able to deny it.

2. He will obey the direction and see God's intervention.

3. The Holy Spirit will impress him to initiate prayer at least once during this time of intercession.

4. He will begin a personal time of prayer with God.

5. He will see prayer as an opportunity rather than an obligation.

Add any additional prayer requests for him.

_____

_____

_____

Reflection on your prayer and fasting time:

_____

_____

_____

God's revelation to you today:

_____

_____

_____

Praise and Thanksgiving:

_____

_____

_____

Pray to your Father

in the secret place.

Matthew 6:6

Day 7

DESIRE FOR TRUTH

John 8:32 — And you shall know the truth, and the truth shall make you free.

I N TODAY'S CULTURE, TRUTH is a moving target. What used to be concrete is now quicksand, constantly shifting to the whims and wishes of the loudest voices. In the past, there was a clear line between truth and lies. And it was universal. Now, I get to have my own personalized "truth," and so do you.

When I decide "my truth" no longer fits what I want to do next, then I get to change it, and no one can refute it.

The Bible is very clear #1 Jesus is the TRUTH [John 14:6], and #2 Jesus NEVER changes [Hebrews 13:8]. In a world that changes with the sunrise and the sunset, the only solid foundation we have is a God who embodies truth and never changes. And though many believe His truth creates bondage, the fact is only His truth sets us free.

For the past six days, we have prayed for the one entrusted to your intercession to allow God's Light to enter in, for the emptiness he feels to be filled by God, for him to experience real joy and recognize it is from God, to experience God and His love differently, to be grateful for all God has done already, and to begin a personal prayer life. Those are all critical aspects of transforming a life. But in the absence of surrender to the power of Biblical truth, those can leave a person feeling better, but not whole.

Write a personal reflection about your beloved so you can be specific when you intercede on his behalf. You can take pieces of the example as appropriate and add different aspects that apply to him.

(Example) He has lived in bondage for most of his life because he wanted to live in **his** truth. Although he studies the Bible consistently, he has not allowed the truth to become a paradigm-shifting mindset. Truth transforms how we see and interact with everything, everyone, everywhere. But it hasn't changed how he views the world, God, religion, success, marriage, parenting, etc., and he has rejected it. That rejection has kept him in bondage to only the "truth" he can create in his mind.

Reflection on your beloved:

————————————————————————————

————————————————————————————

————————————————————————————

————————————————————————————

On Day 7, let us pray (as applicable) that:

1. God will demonstrate unquestionably His Word is trustworthy.

2. He will allow God to transform his life through His truth.

3. He will allow the truths he knows to become the truths that he lives.

4. He will escape his self-imposed prison when he receives the Truth of Christ.

5. God will give him direction and purpose based on his surrender to the Truth.

Add any additional prayer requests for him.

Reflection on your prayer and fasting time:

God's revelation to you today:

Praise and Thanksgiving:

The truth shall

make you free.

John 8:32

Day 8

FROM SICKNESS TO WHOLENESS

Psalm 147:3 — He heals the brokenhearted and binds up their wounds.

I LOVED PLAYING SPORTS when I was growing up and was always playing outside. Although I was never clumsy, I had a few injuries in my time. One time, I was playing first base for my school softball team, and a ball went to my left. I ran to get it even though it was a foul and ran into the barbed wire fence. I tore up my stomach and legs and had to sit on the bench for the remainder of the game. That was bad, but the most significant injury I had was playing basketball. I tore the ACL in my right knee and had to have surgery in 1995 to repair it. Otherwise, I could not safely play anything again.

Most of my accidents have faded from memory along with the scars that initially came with them. And none of them influence how I live today. What strikes me now, however, is one of those scars came from the hurt, but the other came from the healing.

It is rare for any individual to reach adulthood without experiencing some emotional wounds. Sin leaves no one unscathed by the hurt of disempowering words directed at us as children; neglectful, abusive, or absent parents; degrading teachers; taunting schoolmates; dismissive lovers; or trauma inflicted upon our physical body leaving our emotional self in tatters. Some of those hurts fade from memory. Others never will. But, when improperly treated, the scars produced by those wounds will close and appear healed, but under the surface, it influences almost everything we do and every choice we make from the point of injury.

But scars come from both an injury and healing. Dealing with emotional hurt, especially deep traumas, can be painful in the moment and can cause scars, but these are healing scars. When I hurt my knee, no one could see the ligament tear on the inside, but they could see the limp caused by the pain. After the surgery, the limp gradually went away but left a scar that remains twenty-four years later. The scar reminds me I am healed.

Many people refuse to address their emotional injuries and though we can't see the tear on the inside, we see the relational limp on the outside and it impacts how they live.

Write a personal reflection about your beloved so you can be specific when you intercede on his behalf. You can take pieces of the example as appropriate and add different aspects that apply to him.

(Example) He has been hurt a lot in his life. Mental and medical illnesses in his home of origin have created a lot of pain in him and his family. Although he recognizes it intellectually, he has not allowed himself to accept it emotionally. Until he does, he will refuse to do the work to be healed. He will have scars of injury rather than of healing.

Reflection on your beloved:

As we begin week 2, let us pray (as applicable) that:

1. He will acknowledge he has a "limp" and seek healing.

2. He will not run from the emotional treatment that needs to take place for him to heal.

3. God will make Himself known to him as the Great Physician and the Comforter.

4. God will heal his broken heart and bind up his wounds.

5. He will be set free from the pain and the memory of past hurts.

Add any additional prayer requests for him.

_____

_____

Reflection on your prayer and fasting time:

_____

_____

God's revelation to you today:

_____

_____

Praise and Thanksgiving:

_____

_____

He heals

the brokenhearted.

Psalm 147:3

Day 9

PRICELESS IN HIS EYES

John 3:16 — For God so loved the world that He gave His only begotten Son, that whoever believes in Him should not perish but have everlasting life.

ONE SCAR RESULTING FROM unhealed emotional hurt is a diminished sense of self-worth. This used to be considered a teen issue they would grow out of and be okay. Instead, they grew up and became adults who have no belief in their worth and who make choices daily, subtly, and blatantly, giving more evidence of unbelief.

The problem is the world has taught us to "look inside of ourselves" for the source of value. When we do, we see little reason to dispense with our negative image of self.

As Christians, however, we recognize our worth is not centered on us. It can't be. In and of ourselves, life follows the same pattern: we enter from sin, live in sin, and die from sin.

Certainly, in the middle of the cycle, many are "good" and do "good" things and become successful. And for those, it merits them self-worth, esteem, and respect. But as soon as they fail, lose their success, or do something bad, their self-worth tumbles. When worth centers upon me, what I do, who I am, and how I feel about myself, the source is ever-changing. Therefore, my worth is on a rollercoaster through life, never having a constant foundation.

God's view of us, the value he has placed on us, and the price He paid for us is the only true, unchanging measure from which we can derive worth. Adam was created in His image and despite sin, the vestiges of His image remain in us. We are children of the God and King of heaven and earth, which makes us princes and princesses. God sent Jesus, His beloved Son, to live in an evil-infested world, to be tortured by the very presence of sin, and to die at the hands of sinners, all so your beloved could have a chance at life.

The value of a thing is determined by the price someone will pay. It's our "God-worth."

Write a personal reflection about your beloved so you can be specific when you intercede on his behalf. You can take pieces of the example as appropriate and add different aspects that apply to him.

(Example) He judges his worth by the world's measuring stick and comes up wanting in his mind. After worldly success slipped away, the voice got louder and louder, overwhelming him, and drawing the darkness to himself. Every morning he wakes up to chase down his self-worth, and every night he returns with an empty heart because he is chasing the wrong source.

Reflection on your beloved:

_____

_____

_____

On Day 9, let us pray (as applicable) that:

1. He will recognize value can never be derived from who we are or what we do.

2. He will learn the truth about his "God-worth" and rest in this truth.

3. He will stop chasing success and start seeking fulfillment.

4. God will manifest Himself to him, for him, and in him so your beloved can see his value to Him.

5. God will become his source, so his heart will always be full and his value sure.

Add any additional prayer requests for him.

_____

_____

_____

Reflection on your prayer and fasting time:

_____

_____

_____

God's revelation to you today:

_____

_____

_____

Praise and Thanksgiving:

_____

_____

_____

God loved

so He gave!

John 3:16

Day 10

MIRROR OF THE SOUL

*Lamentations 3:40 — Let us search out and examine our ways
and, turn back to the Lord.*

As a social work student, I learned a lot about self-awareness during my two years of graduate school. No subject escaped the keen eye of self-reflection and demanded a paper sharing those reflections. If I am serving others and trying to help them change, make different decisions, recognize their unhealthy behavior, alter it, and identify their impact on others, I must be able to do the same in my life. That doesn't mean I always follow through on change, it just means I know what I need to change.

Knowing is half the battle.

The Bible is clear the only person I should examine is myself. I can certainly see the fruits of others and know something is problematic with their tree. However, my responsibility is to see myself, know where I am, and ask God to transform me as I walk with Him. Self-reflection allows me to see the truth about myself and to change the only person I have control over...me. The bonus of self-reflection is it also lets me see other people more clearly as my lens has been upgraded. And it is interesting every time I have done this in my life, my relationships have changed. Hmmm...

Write a personal reflection about your beloved so you can be specific when you intercede on his behalf. You can take pieces of the example as appropriate and add different aspects that apply to him.

(Example) He often avoids seeing his behavior as contributing to negative situations, disappointing outcomes, and rocky relationships in his life. This results from unhealed hurt and the impact on his self-worth. Refusing to see himself honestly, to own his weaknesses, accept responsibility, and commit to change may help him maintain a semblance of esteem, but it has left his life and relationships in shambles.

Reflection on your beloved:

_____

_____

_____

On Day 10, let us pray (as applicable) that:

1. He will take the time to examine himself, his life, work, relationships, family, spiritual life, etc. and honestly see where he needs to turn around.

2. He will begin the difficult process of admitting his weakness and taking responsibility for his role in creating some issues he is currently experiencing in all areas of his life.

3. God will show him a true picture of himself through God's eyes.

4. God will block any of the enemy's attempts to distort the picture he sees so he becomes more disheartened.

5. God will bring him comfort and encouragement, so he is hopeful and not hopeless.

6. He will see God walking with him through his process and guiding him through his transformation.

Add any additional prayer requests for him.

_____

_____

_____

Reflection on your prayer and fasting time:

_____

_____

_____

God's revelation to you today:

_____

_____

_____

Praise and Thanksgiving:

_____

_____

_____

Examine your ways

and turn back to the Lord.

Lamentations 3:40

Day 11

SURRENDERING ANGER

Proverbs 16:32 — He who is slow to anger is better than the mighty, and he who rules his spirit than he who takes a city.

WE LIVE IN A perpetually angry world. Vitriolic battles pervade social media as invisible people release their deep-seated anger and bitterness at an unknown person who dares to disagree with their opinion. Children bully classmates literally to suicide. Formerly inseparable lovers pepper their now despised exes with insults and hatred. In addition to political animosity, mass shootings, racial division, and countless other areas of disunity, anger on a societal scale is inevitable. Many people believe that releasing their anger is freedom. They celebrate getting things off their chest. Yet, the truth is real liberty doesn't come from venting it, but from surrendering it.

Despite the current environment, God calls his followers to a higher standard. The Bible repeatedly describes those who are quick to anger as foolish and deems the man or woman who can manage their anger as wise. This is no small feat in a world from which the Holy Spirit appears to be slowly withdrawing and people are losing their minds to demonic control. And yet, we are required to uproot the spirit of anger and bitterness resting in our soul and surrender it to God because it does not produce the righteousness of God.

If we don't identify the source of our anger and surrender it, we will be destructive in our relationships and trapped in an emotional prison of our own making. In addition, we become part of the problem God is trying to solve in the world rather than part of sharing His solution with those who don't know the truth of salvation and sanctification.

Write a personal reflection about your beloved so you can be specific when you intercede on his behalf. You can take pieces of the example as appropriate and add different aspects that apply to him.

(Example) He carries anger and bitterness in his heart for a lifetime of hurts, small and great, real, and imagined. On a good day, you will never know he has not moved on from issues between you all. However, on a bad day, the depth of those feelings will show up and there will be no doubt of where he remains. These displays are not without collateral damage to both the victim and the perpetrator. Unless he can identify, face, and let go of the anger he carries for so many things, he will remain a prisoner of his mind, replaying old slights like television reruns.

Reflection on your beloved:

_____

_____

_____

Today, on Day 11, let us pray (as applicable) that:

1. God will show him a clear picture of how destructive anger is and how he has created a toxic environment for those close to him because of it.

2. He will identify the areas where he is carrying anger and bitterness.

3. He will express a desire to be free from the bondage of his anger.

4. As He surrenders, God will remove the memory of those hurts from him so he can be free.

5. He will feel a God-given peace.

6. God will show him how to be angry for the right reasons and not sin.

7. God will teach him how to rule his emotions even when he is justified in his feelings.

Add any additional prayer requests for him.

_____

_____

_____

Reflection on your prayer and fasting time:

_____

_____

_____

God's revelation to you today:

_____

_____

_____

Praise and Thanksgiving:

_____

_____

_____

He who is slow to anger

is better than the mighty.

Proverbs 16:32

Day 12

WELLNESS FROM WITHIN

1 Corinthians 6:19, 20 — What? Know ye not that your body is the temple of the Holy Ghost, which is in you, which ye have of God, and ye are not your own? For ye are bought with a price: therefore, glorify God in your body, and in your spirit, which are God's.

LOW FAT, NO FAT, high carb, high fat, HIIT, orange zone, six meals a day, one meal a day, no meals...argh...Calgon take me away!!! Society is constantly coming out with a new health craze in nutrition, exercise, supplements, scheduling, tracking, etc. And everyone jumps on board and goes hard until it fizzles out and we are on to the next thing to get us fit and in shape.

But the focus here is not health, but fitness, which is different. Ultimately, it is about how I look on the outside rather than how well I function on the inside. But even current science realizes the importance of holistic health. It impacts not just the external appearance, but the internal capacity.

Health is about the body, mind, and spirit.

The Bible reminds us more than once our body is not our property, but the temple of God in the person of the Holy Spirit. We have no idea how it works or what it means practically. It must be important if the Holy Spirit impressed Paul to include it in the scriptures. We are the dwelling place of God, which means He has a right to us in three ways. He created us. He redeemed us. He lives in us.

We have more responsibility to care for our bodies as God's home than we do for the physical homes in which we reside.

Write a personal reflection about your beloved so you can be specific when you intercede on his behalf. You can take pieces of the example as appropriate and add different aspects that apply to him.

(**Example**) He has lived in an unhealthy manner for most, if not all, of his life. Habits developed in childhood have followed him through adulthood and it has been detrimental to him. Lack of sleep, poor eating habits, little consistent exercise, poor stress management, always rushing around and many other things have contributed to the lack of wellness he experiences. This impacts his ability to think clearly. It makes him easily frustrated and angered, and it's difficult to find moments of peace to connect spiritually.

Reflection on your beloved:

Today, Day 12, let us pray (as applicable) that:

1. He will recognize the importance of his health and wellness to God, himself, and his family.

2. He will take at least one action per day that moves him toward wellness.

3. He will trade one bad health habit for one good health habit within this 30-day intercession.

4. He will schedule one fun, stress-relieving activity for himself each week.

5. God will impress him to participate with his family on the journey to health and wellness.

Add any additional prayer requests for him.

_____

_____

_____

Reflection on your prayer and fasting time:

_____

_____

_____

God's revelation to you today:

_____

_____

_____

Praise and Thanksgiving:

_____

_____

_____

Your body is the temple

of the Holy Spirit.

1 Corinthians 6:19

Day 13

THE POWER OF VALUES

Psalm 51:6 — Behold you desire truth in the inward parts, and in the hidden part
you will make me to know wisdom.

I N OUR CURRENT CULTURE, there is a movement toward holistic growth
that is, in a sense, a rebellion against the consumerism of the last generation.
Within the movement is the recognition that our values determine our mindset,
life choices, and ultimately, the life we have. How I spend my time, what I do with
money, what I am consistent with, what excites me, who I associate with, what I
am disciplined about, what I talk about, etc. are ways I reflect my values.

No matter what I say, if I don't change my behaviors to match my expressed
values, it means nothing.

Who I am, how I live, what I do, my relationships, the trajectory of my work,
my health, my financial state, my spiritual strength, etc. are perfect reflections
of my values, despite my protestations to the contrary. Many of us struggle with
cognitive dissonance in our lives. Who we say we want to be and who we try to
impress the world we are does not match the reality of who we are and how we
live. Our values are manifested in the story of our life, good and bad.

The Bible is a perfect reflection of God's values. Many people incorrectly look
at the Bible as a rule book in which we are told what to do and then penalized
for disobeying and rewarded for obeying. The Bible includes commandments
that are prescriptive of how God wants us to live so we can enjoy our best life,

even in this world of sin. However, the Bible in its totality is a narrative. It is descriptive of our Heavenly Father and demonstrates His values through His interest, interaction, engagement, intercession, and redemption of fallen man. In the story, we get to see how God values relationships. He walked and talked with Adam and Eve face to face before sin.

After the Fall, He approached with mercy first and then grace. He was long-suffering with the evil of man and fought hard and long to get them to turn from their sin before judgment came. He wanted reconciliation. God demonstrated inexplicable love when He allowed His Son to come to this earth, live amid this evil world, and then die for people who rejected Him.

God's values are perfectly manifested in the Biblical narrative of Him.

Write a personal reflection about your beloved so you can be specific when you intercede on his behalf. You can take pieces of the example as appropriate and add different aspects that apply to him.

(**Example**) His life reflects his values. His marriage, parenting, business, friendships, health, wealth, and spirituality are a narrative of what he designed them to be. His satisfaction, displeasure, joy, or frustration with any of those aspects are not based on other people, but on himself.

Reflection on your beloved:

On Day 13, let us pray (as applicable) that:

1. He will recognize the life he has is the life he has crafted based on his values.

2. He will do an honest, serious assessment of his values and adjust to fit the life he wants.

3. He will not waste time grieving what is but will focus on what will be.

4. God's values will become the template for him as he reconstructs his own.

5. God will give him direction, commitment, and perseverance in this process.

6. God will strengthen him during those difficult times of change that will come.

7. He will see some immediate improvements in his life because of changing what he values.

Add any additional prayer requests for him.

>———————————————————————————————————<

>———————————————————————————————————<

>———————————————————————————————————<

>———————————————————————————————————<

Reflection on your prayer and fasting time:

>———————————————————————————————————<

>———————————————————————————————————<

>———————————————————————————————————<

>———————————————————————————————————<

God's revelation to you today:

> ―――

> ―――

> ―――

> ―――

Praise and Thanksgiving:

> ―――

> ―――

> ―――

> ―――

You desire truth

in the inward parts.

Psalm 51:6

Day 14

GUIDANCE AND GROWTH

Proverbs 8:33 — Hear instruction, and be wise, and do not disdain it.

ALTHOUGH SEEKING THERAPY IS much more accepted than in previous periods, some men tend to remain resistant to the idea. "I'm not crazy," "Counseling is for weak men," or "I ain't getting ready to tell my business to a stranger" are some of the most common refrains heard in opposition to the suggestion that someone sees a therapist or counselor. Yet, men face an unprecedented level of stressors in the world today, in addition to the profound history of issues from the past. It would be significantly helpful for them to talk about these things and process them with a neutral person. The goal is to help them effectively move past the issues, so they no longer impact their current life, behavior, and relationships.

Many men are still resistant to this idea.

The Bible has quite the opposite view of people who seek counsel rather than trying to deal with concerns or challenges on their own. Solomon, the wisest man who ever lived, talked much about getting counsel in Proverbs. He is a father who gives advice to his son and tells him seeking counsel is a good thing. Those who hear instruction and receive correction are the wise ones, and it is the foolish who reject instruction, advice, or counsel and only listen to themselves. The point Solomon makes is counsel, advice, or instruction should be from a wise person and not someone who is failing in similar areas.

Prayer is critical, Bible study is necessary, and friends are important. But sometimes the things we have gone through or are going through require us to sit down with a counselor, coach, or therapist. We can get it out of our heads, process it, analyze it, examine our current life considering those traumas. Then we can employ tools to help us leave those issues in the past and mitigate its impact on our current behavior.

Write a personal reflection about your beloved so you can be specific when you intercede on his behalf. You can take pieces of the example as appropriate and add different aspects that apply to him.

(**Example**) He has resisted the idea of counseling as a waste of time even though he has depression and has a strong family history of mental illness. And the issues keeping him in bondage remain.

Reflection on your beloved:

_____

_____

_____

On Day 14, let us pray (as applicable) that:

1. He will see value in seeking counseling.

2. He will commit to going and staying with a Christian therapist for individual counseling until he is emotionally healthy.

3. God will give him discernment in selecting a counselor to walk with him on this journey.

4. He will talk about and address the issues keeping him in bondage.

5. He will follow through on what the counselor instructs him to do.

6. God will comfort him, and give him strength and peace in, thru, and after the process.

Add any additional prayer requests for him.

_____

_____

_____

Reflection on your prayer and fasting time:

_____

_____

_____

God's revelation to you today:

_____

_____

_____

Praise and Thanksgiving:

_____

_____

_____

Hear instruction

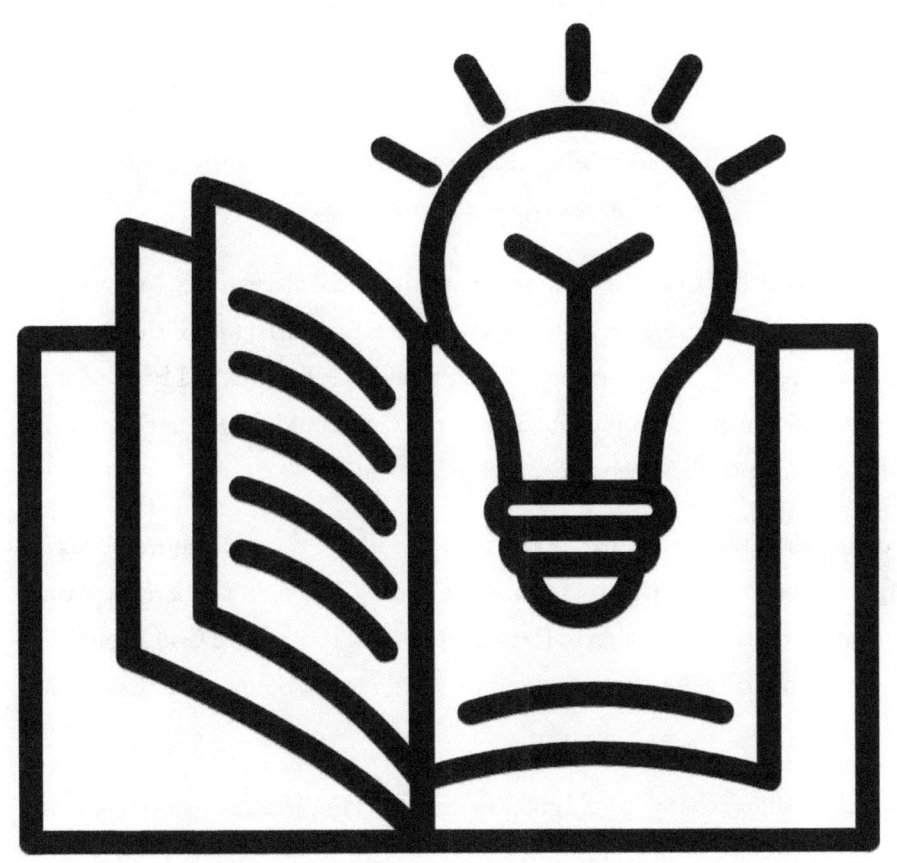

and be wise.

Proverbs 8:33

Day 15

To Forgive, Divine

1 John 1:9 — If we confess our sins, He is faithful and just to forgive us our sins and to cleanse us from all unrighteousness.

THE BIBLE IS CLEAR if we confess our sins, God will forgive us. In one sense, it is one of the clearest and easiest scriptures to understand and implement. And yet, for many years of my life, I didn't believe it for myself. I believed it in general and for other people, but I doubted God could forgive me for all my terrible sins, especially when I kept repeating them.

It didn't seem real to me that God would just throw those sins into the sea of forgetfulness, and I would have a clean slate once again. I didn't believe He wasn't frustrated and tired of having to forgive me. I would try to give God a couple of days to "cool off" before coming to confess and repent. Sounds funny now, but it was real.

My feelings didn't change until I got personal with Him and understood the truth that He is a Divine Other. He is Love. And His faithfulness to His Word is never failing.

The forgiveness of God through the life, death, and resurrection of Jesus is the greatest gift ever given. Made available for all who desire it and confess our sins to Him. It is free to us, but we must recognize and accept it to get the benefit of freedom from our guilt and shame through forgiveness. But when we recognize we need it, God has promised His faithfulness and justice will extend to us every single time we do wrong. He then continues to cleanse from sin and all other desires to sin through sanctification.

Forgiveness is a divine act. The Bible commands us to forgive because it is an act of kindness and forbearance toward our brothers and sisters. It also reminds us this is how Christ treated us. His forgiveness is freely given to those who desire it. If we want to reflect Christ to those in our lives, we must forgive others the same way He forgave us. We experience the freedom that comes with being forgiven to truly embrace the role of forgiver the way the Bible commands it. It cannot be done grudgingly or reluctantly but with an open heart of love toward the guilty ones. This can only be done through the Holy Spirit.

Write a personal reflection about your beloved so you can be specific when you intercede on his behalf. You can take pieces of the example as appropriate and add different aspects that apply to him.

(**Example**) He doesn't forgive people who have wronged him. He will bury it inside, especially if he must continue to relate to the person in his daily life. However, the memory of the offense, small or great, rests just below the surface of his pleasant and sociable exterior and, if triggered, will be recounted as if it happened yesterday. There are many reasons this is so; past hurts, insecurity, and his lack of experience with God's forgiveness are the main ones. We have asked God to move in the other areas and we have faith He is and will continue to. But if He doesn't accept he has sinned against God and then seek God's forgiveness for his sin, he will never be forgiven nor be a genuine forgiver.

Reflection on your beloved:

As we begin Week 3, Day 15 let us pray (as applicable) that:

1. God will show him a true picture of himself, and why he needs a Savior.

2. He will see himself as a sinner in need of forgiveness from God and ask for it.

3. God will allow him to feel a weight lifted from his soul when he receives the forgiveness he needs from God.

4. He will accept the forgiveness God gives and let go of any guilt he is carrying.

5. God will give him a forgiving heart so he can give others the experience God gave him.

Add any additional prayer requests for him.

—————————————————————————————————

—————————————————————————————————

—————————————————————————————————

—————————————————————————————————

Reflection on your prayer and fasting time:

—————————————————————————————————

—————————————————————————————————

—————————————————————————————————

—————————————————————————————————

God's revelation to you today:

_____

_____

_____

_____

Praise and Thanksgiving:

_____

_____

_____

_____

If we confess our sins

He is faithful to forgive.

1 John 1:9

Day 16

REBUILDING BRIDGES

2 Corinthians 7:9, 10 — Now I rejoice, not that you were made sorry, but that your sorrow led to repentance. For you were made sorry in a godly manner, that you might suffer loss from us in nothing. For godly sorrow produces repentance leading to salvation, not to be regretted; but the sorrow of the world produces death.

IT REQUIRES HUMILITY TO ask for forgiveness when we have committed a fault against another person. When we sin against God, we occasionally act a bit casual about it because we don't see His pain and hear His hurt. Getting on our knees, or not, and asking for forgiveness from our Father sometimes doesn't carry the weight that it should because we know God promises to forgive if we repent.

We don't have that assurance with another person, and seeking forgiveness comes with risk to our hearts and egos. The humility required to accept the risk is often the biggest hurdle we must overcome. Yet without it, it is impossible to come with genuine sorrow for the wrong we have committed and ask for forgiveness and restoration. No one accepts an arrogant apology or flippant request for forgiveness. Why? It minimizes the responsibility of the offender. Or makes it seem it wasn't a big deal. As if we are apologizing only because they are making the issue bigger than it was.

Love withers and dies in the absence of mutual genuine sorrow for wrongs committed against the other.

The Bible gives a mandate to those who claim to be followers of Christ to forgive everyone all the time. If we cannot forgive, we will exclude ourselves from the blessing of God's forgiveness. It is a risk none of us truly can take, considering how often we need the forgiveness of God. We must adopt God's heart and extend forgiveness. We also must love enough to humble ourselves to seek forgiveness so love can grow.

Write a personal reflection about your beloved so you can be specific when you intercede on his behalf. You can take pieces of the example as appropriate and add different aspects that apply to him.

(**Example**) He has caused as much hurt as he has suffered. But he refuses to see the damage he has caused. He deflects responsibility for his harmful reactions by justifying his behavior, excusing his choices, or minimizing his wrongs. All these responses are demonstrations of worldly sorrow, which leads to death. Death of love, death of trust, death of joy, death of peace, death of relationships. Yesterday, we prayed He would see himself as a sinner and seek forgiveness from God.

Reflection on your beloved:

_____

_____

_____

Today as we pray on Day 16, let us pray (as applicable) that:

1. God will humble him in this process so he will see his sins against others and feel godly sorrow, not guilt.

2. He will ask forgiveness from you with true, humble repentance for the many ways he has broken your heart.

3. He will ask forgiveness from any other family member or friend he has hurt with his attitude, words, or actions.

4. God will resurrect love, trust, joy, peace, and relationships in his life as he repents and seeks reconciliation.

Add any additional prayer requests for him.

_____

_____

_____

Reflection on your prayer and fasting time:

_____

_____

_____

God's revelation to you today:

_____

_____

_____

Praise and Thanksgiving:

_____

_____

_____

Godly sorrow

produces repentance.

2 Corinthians 7:9, 10

Day 17

THE GIFT OF FORGIVENESS

Luke 17:4 — And if he sins against you seven times in a day, and seven times in a day returns to you, saying, "I repent," you shall forgive him.

I T REQUIRES HUMILITY TO offer forgiveness to someone who has hurt you. When we are the ones who have been wronged, it is easy to be arrogant and keep the "upper hand" in the relationship by continuously reminding the person of their wrong or using their guilt to manipulate them into surrendering to our will. This is most prevalent in marriage but is used in parenting, friendships, and work relationships. It is easy when you are the victim of hurt, to forget yesterday you were, or tomorrow you will be, the perpetrator.

This self-righteous approach to relationships creates resentment, discontentment, and uncertainty in the unforgiven party and causes them to either walk on eggshells or become indifferent because they are never sure of their status with the injured party.

The Bible rejects this manner of relationship management in the strongest terms. We are repeatedly reminded as followers of God we will remain unforgiven if we don't forgive everyone, for everything, every time. Unforgiveness equals lostness. The gift given to us by Christ needs to be given to everyone in our lives when they need it. When we fail to forgive because we refuse to humble ourselves and let go of the upper hand against a brother or sister in Christ, the Bible reminds us our fall will come soon enough.

However, when we recognize we are sinners saved by only the grace of God and we sin against God far more than anyone could ever sin against us, humility comes a lot easier, and the domino effect is a greater willingness to forgive others for their wrongs.

Write a personal reflection about your beloved so you can be specific when you intercede on his behalf. You can take pieces of the example as appropriate and add different aspects that apply to him.

(**Example**) He has suffered many hurts in this life. But he hasn't forgiven. We asked God to give him forgiveness so he would finally understand the beauty and freedom of it and the desire to share it with others. We believe God is answering the prayer in his heart to which only God has access. We have asked him to seek forgiveness from those he has hurt because until he humbles himself before a person he has wronged, the tendency to keep the upper hand may linger.

Reflection on your beloved:

_____

_____

_____

Today, on Day 17, let us pray (as applicable) that:

1. God will soften his hardened heart so all arrogance, self-righteousness, fear, and pride will be destroyed, and he will live, love, and walk in humility.

2. He will forgive everyone, for everything he has been holding onto.

3. God will bring reconciliation in all his relationships as he surrenders his "right" to be mad.

4. God will remove the memory of those hurts from everyone and put them into the "sea of forgetfulness."

Add any additional prayer requests for him.

_____

_____

_____

Reflection on your prayer and fasting time:

_____

_____

_____

God's revelation to you today:

_____

_____

_____

Praise and Thanksgiving:

_____

_____

_____

If he says, "I repent"

you shall forgive him.

Luke 17:4

Day 18

BEYOND STEREOTYPES

1 Corinthians 13:11 — When I was a child, I spoke as a child, I understood as a child, I thought as a child; but when I became a man, I put away childish things.

MANHOOD, AS DEFINED BY the world, is a distorted, demonic juxtaposition of independent, invulnerable, sexual conqueror, provider, self-confident, and tough. Males who don't embrace these stereotypical behaviors are labeled as weak. This starts as early as childhood and influences the mindset and behavior of boys into adulthood. But attempting to incorporate all these traits in his life can leave a man feeling empty on the inside while maintaining on the outside. Independence is a myth keeping men from asking for help. Invulnerability forces them to suppress their emotions and become unbalanced. The sexual conqueror diminishes his capacity to bond with his wife, even when he wants to. The provider is unable to disconnect his manhood from his bank account and breaks down in the absence of financial evidence of his "success." Self-confidence makes man's accomplishments the source of his worth and this becomes a rollercoaster based on his assessment of himself from day to day. Toughness doesn't allow for compassion and inhibits true intimacy.

Is there any wonder why men who embrace this paradigm, consciously or subconsciously, struggle to have healthy, intimate relationships?

The Bible provides a counter definition for manhood and provides a picture of the perfect man in the person of Jesus Christ. We can see Him walking the earth, living in the body of a human man, and teaching us by word and example what godly manhood looks like. He was all-powerful, but still asked His three best friends to pray and stay close to Him when the cross was imminent. Christ demonstrated his vulnerability when he wept over Jerusalem and how she had rejected His salvation. He treated with honor and respect all women He interacted with, seeing them as sisters, mothers, and daughters, not objects. Jesus reminded those who said they wanted to follow Him that He was without a home or means to provide, but offered them the best thing ever: Himself. Jesus humbled Himself and directed all glory to His Father, even though He was fully God and had the right to accept the glory. He showed compassion to those who were rejected by the world and the church.

Jesus was the perfect example of manhood.

Write a personal reflection about your beloved so you can be specific when you intercede on his behalf. You can take pieces of the example as appropriate and add different aspects that apply to him.

(**Example**) He has been indoctrinated with the world's picture of manhood. He refuses to seek or accept help. He buries or runs from his emotions and has become unbalanced in his relationships. His pseudo-confidence covers up the depth of insecurity crippling him. And he often lacks empathy and compassion for those closest to him.

Reflection on your beloved:

_____

_____

_____

On Day 18, let us pray (as applicable) that:

1. God will send him a godly friend who is an example of what a true man looks like and how he lives.

2. God will shift his paradigm of manhood from a worldly version to a Biblical version.

3. He will accept help from, and give help to, you and others when necessary.

4. He will be vulnerable to his family and not shut down or shut them out.

5. He will focus on providing relational security for his family.

6. He will learn humility and compassion.

Add any additional prayer requests for him.

_____

_____

Reflection on your prayer and fasting time:

_____

_____

God's revelation to you today:

_____

_____

Praise and Thanksgiving:

_____

_____

When I became a man,

I put away childish things.

1 Corinthians 13:11

Day 19

BUILDING HAPPILY EVER AFTER

Ephesians 5:28 — So husbands ought to love their own wives as their own bodies; he who loves his wife loves himself.

MARRIAGE IS ONE OF the most significant, influential, and profound human relationships possible. It is the relationship that has the most power over the destiny of the individuals. And yet, marriage, as demonstrated by many in the world and the church, is a distorted, self-gratifying contract, easily broken, either officially or in practice, at the hint of discontent or "irreconcilable difference."

The relative ease with which partners can be, and are dismissed, has had an inestimable negative impact on this world. A divorce is an unfortunate option for many, despite the commitment to "until death do us part." The reasons for this are varied, but the most fundamental reason is the origin and purpose of marriage have been hijacked by Satan to be a man-made idea with a man-glorifying purpose. Most people marry to be happy, to be served, and to have their needs gratified by their spouse. It is a contractual relationship founded on an "if you...then I" mindset.

However, marriage is not a man-made, man-glorifying idea, it is a God-made, God-glorifying covenant.

God is the originator of marriage and set man up on the first blind date ever. God is the ultimate matchmaker and still seeks to be. Marriage, as created by God, is a covenant between two disciples who join their lives to replicate the image of God as a couple and fulfill His mission in the world as one rather than as two. When done in God's way, the kingdom marriage is the source of much joy and fulfillment for the couple and those they influence. A covenant differs greatly from a contract because it doesn't rely on the behavior, choices, or commitment of the other person as a gauge for keeping the covenant.

The covenant marriage is about serving and not being served. It is about becoming the best spouse, not having the best spouse. The kingdom marriage has God at its center and example, and therefore, even if one person gets off track, the covenant directs the choices of the other.

The kingdom marriage is founded on the "even if you...then I still" mindset because the covenant is with God first, then our spouse and He is always faithful.

Write a personal reflection about your beloved so you can be specific when you intercede on his behalf. You can take pieces of the example as appropriate and add different aspects that apply to him.

(**Example**) He has misunderstood the covenantal nature of marriage. It is a temporal, practical, contractual relationship, but not necessarily a divinely appointed relationship with a purpose beyond satisfying earthly needs and wants. Because of this, he has lived in an "if you...then I" contract, rather than leading an "even if you...then I still' covenant.

Reflection on your beloved:

_____

_____

_____

On Day 19, let us pray (as applicable) that:

1. God will give him an understanding of a covenant marriage and how to create it.

2. God will give him a godly man to mentor him to become a husband that unites his family.

3. He will be unselfish in his marriage.

4. He will attend and complete marriage counseling.

5. He will understand covenantal faithfulness and all its facets and implications.

6. God will change his desire and focus on becoming the best husband.

7. God will make him one with his wife.

8. God will reveal to him the kingdom's purpose for marriage.

Add any additional prayer requests for him.

>———————————————————————————————<

>———————————————————————————————<

>———————————————————————————————<

>———————————————————————————————<

Reflection on your prayer and fasting time:

>———————————————————————————————<

>———————————————————————————————<

>———————————————————————————————<

>———————————————————————————————<

God's revelation to you today:

_____

_____

_____

_____

Praise and Thanksgiving:

_____

_____

_____

_____

Husbands love your wives

as your own body.
Ephesians 5:28

Day 20

DONOR OR INVESTOR?

*Proverbs 20:7 — The righteous man walks in his integrity;
his children are blessed after him.*

FATHERHOOD IS ONE OF the few things you can contribute one time and still get to keep the title. A person who jogs one time around their neighborhood, no matter how fast and long they do it, would not be called a runner. Someone who donated to their local charity one time, though appreciated, would not be called a philanthropist. If you went to class for one day, no one would call you a student, nor if you taught one class would anyone deem you a teacher.

Yet a man can make one deposit of sperm that fertilizes an egg, in any random woman, go on his merry way, invest nothing more in or for the child, and still claim the title of father for the rest of his life. And millions of men, or more aptly males, do it every year. A donor can give once; an investor spends his life depositing into what he wants to grow.

Too many men are donors, not investors in the lives of their children.

Being a father, biological or not, plays a critical role in the life of a child. because. From the birth of the child or their entry into their life, a human father represents the Heavenly Father in the lives of their children whether or not they are a believer. At some point in their life, children will likely hear of God, the Father. How they relate to God as Father will be significantly influenced by their experience with their earthly father.

In Genesis 2, our Heavenly Father has provided a template in the creation of Adam, that invested fathers can follow to bless their children. God breathed life into Adam, gave him a home, showed him his purpose, set boundaries, met his needs, and gave him work to do.

Write a personal reflection about your beloved so you can be specific when you intercede on his behalf. You can take pieces of the example as appropriate and add different aspects that apply to him.

(**Example — Biological Father**) He has been a donor rather than an investor in his children's lives. He seems to have embraced a role as a walk-on versus a leading man in their lives. He continues to be emotionally absent while physically present. For the most part, he has left the responsibility for raising his children into healthy, whole, productive, adults to their mother and others. He occasionally donates a ride, a dinner, a gift, or a visit that satisfies an immediate need, but doesn't make daily investments of time, love, discipline, affection, instruction, and direction that nurtures growth for a lifetime.

(**Example — Stepfather**) He may not know it or believe it, but he impacts his stepchildren because of his presence in their lives. He needs to remember even though they may have a biological father, as a stepfather, he can still influence them and their decisions. He needs to live so his influence is positive. He still needs to make investments of time, love, affection, guidance, and support to nurture their growth for a lifetime.

Reflection on your beloved:

_____

_____

_____

On Day 20, let us pray (as applicable) that:

1. God will show him how important his role is as a father or stepfather.

2. God will show him where he fits in his children's lives.

3. He will meet his children's needs for his time, love, affection, guidance, and support.

4. He will represent God the Father to all his children.

5. He will be a consistent and present partner in helping and supporting his children.

Add any additional prayer requests for him.

_____

_____

_____

Reflection on your prayer and fasting time:

_____

_____

_____

God's revelation to you today:

_____

_____

_____

Praise and Thanksgiving:

His children are

blessed after him.

Proverbs 20:7

Day 21

SOUL TIES

Proverbs 12:26 — The righteous should choose his friends carefully, for the way of the wicked leads them astray.

BESIDES A SPOUSE, FRIENDS have the greatest influence on the choices and ultimate destiny of an individual. It is often repeated we are the sum of the five people closest to us, and this is true whether they are good or bad. We may agree as it relates to children or teenagers. We believe them to be subject to peer pressure and so we warn them about various dangers to keep them on the right path. However, adults are just as susceptible to the influence or pressure of friends as young people. Our decisions are just as empowering or destructive.

If I evaluate my life and find I am stuck in a destructive pattern or place, I should also assess the lives of my friends. When we wish to progress, having progressive friends who push us can be the key to unlocking the door to growth. However, when we are stuck, the easiest thing we can do is stay connected to people who don't challenge us to grow. In their company, there will be no progress, but also no judgment.

The Bible says followers of Christ should choose friends who are likewise disciples.

They don't have to be and think exactly like us, but they need to be going in the same direction, toward Christ. When this is true, behaviors, choices, and plans we set will be led by the Spirit and supported and assisted by godly friends.

Anytime we choose to live against the principles and guidelines of God, our choice will be admonished and/or rebuked. A faithful, godly friend will never support unhealthy behaviors even as they continue to love and support us. And because of this, it will become uncomfortable for us to do the wrong thing. We will either choose to end the friendship or choose to change the behavior.

Write a personal reflection about your beloved so you can be specific when you intercede on his behalf. You can take pieces of the example as appropriate and add distinct aspects that apply to him.

(**Example**) He has friends, but in many critical ways, they are stuck as well. They don't challenge him on his thinking and behavior when it is negative or unproductive. He needs to develop friendships with men who think from a godly perspective and will encourage him to grow in the areas where he is weak.

Reflection on your beloved:

>————————————————————————————————————<

>————————————————————————————————————<

>————————————————————————————————————<

>————————————————————————————————————<

On Day 21, let us pray (as applicable) that:

1. God will create a desire in him to establish productive friendships.

2. God will help him get unstuck through his relationship with positive friends.

3. He will be a positive influence on his friends.

4. He will listen to his friends who pull him up and correct him when he is wrong.

5. He will be a friend who pulls others up and checks them when they are wrong.

6. God will give him wisdom and discernment in his friendships.

Add any additional prayer requests for him.

>——<

>——<

>——<

>——<

Reflection on your prayer and fasting time:

>——<

>——<

>——<

>——<

God's revelation to you today:

>——<

>——<

>——<

>——<

Praise and Thanksgiving:

>——<

>——<

>——<

>——<

The righteous should

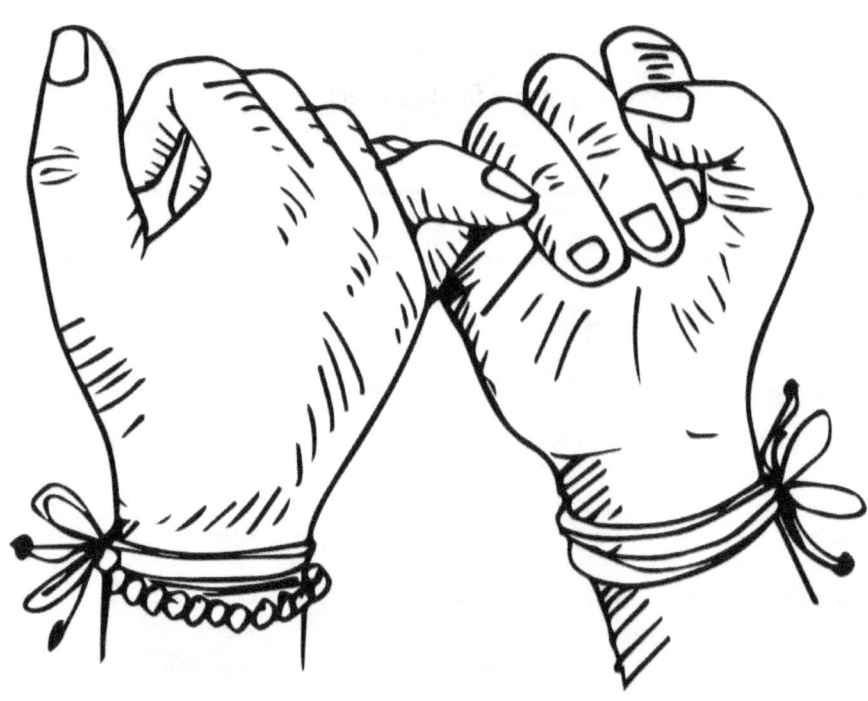

choose friends carefully.

Proverbs 12:26

Day 22

Breaking Chains

Romans 7:19, 20 — For the good that I will to do, I do not do; but the evil I will not do, that I practice. Now if I do what I will not to do, it is no longer I who do it, but sin that dwells in me.

ADDICTION IS BOTH A physical and a psychological compulsion to consume a chemical, drug, activity, or substance. It used to be discussed primarily as it related to alcohol and drug use, and the interventions focused on physical cravings. It didn't take long to realize something more was happening within a person to cause them to destroy life, limbs, health, marriages, children, careers, money, etc. in pursuit of destructive habits.

There are growing reports and manifestations of addiction to things other than drugs or alcohol; pornography, video games, smartphones, gambling, and even food made the list of things people use to manage or suppress their emotions. The world expanded its focus on the psychological aspects of these strongholds and tried to help individuals recover for good. And though success increased, we are not winning the war as a society.

There is a critical missing piece to the world's understanding of addiction.

The Bible provides the missing piece. This dependency doesn't just involve the body and mind. It takes the soul and emotions, too. God asks us to love Him with all our heart, soul, mind, and strength. This stronghold is a thief whose purpose as a weapon of Satan is to steal, kill, and destroy our hearts, souls, minds, and strength. Our affections become alienated from God and others. God is removed from the center of our life and replaced with something or someone else. It steals our minds by diminishing our ability to make wise decisions, use or hear sound reasoning, or process situations accurately or effectively. Compulsion steals our strength by destroying our health and wellness, even when the craving is not for something ingestible.

The addiction thief may come, but God says He has come as well, and He still offers abundant life to those trapped by the sin they don't want to do but have not overcome.

Write a personal reflection about your beloved so you can be specific when you intercede on his behalf. You can take pieces of the example as appropriate and add different aspects that apply to him.

(**Example**) He may have more than one addiction. This is not uncommon. Sometimes these habits sneak in; sometimes we open the door wide and allow them in. How it happened for him is a bell that cannot be unrung. Yet, no matter the entry point, the result is the same. It has stolen his heart, mind, soul, and strength. But God can restore it all if he surrenders.

Reflection on your beloved:

On Day 22, let us pray (as applicable) that:

1. God will break through the fog and give him the ability to make one reasoned, discerning, wise decision this week to resist the addictive behavior and start a new neural pathway.

2. God will show up and pierce his heart with the love addiction can never provide.

3. He will have a moment of clarity that exposes the emptiness of his spirit but points Him to God rather than the addictive behavior.

4. He will give God the chance to be the Lord in one major decision in his life before the end of the intercession.

5. He will wake up alert, rested, vibrant, and strong when he says "no" to the flesh and sluggish, tired, foggy, and in pain when he says "yes", and he will recognize the difference.

6. He will address his addictions in counseling and actively seek recovery.

Add any additional prayer requests for him.

Reflection on your prayer and fasting time:

God's revelation to you today:

Praise and Thanksgiving:

The good I want to do

I keep failing to do.

Romans 7:19, 20

Day 23

THE BATTLE FOR HIS MIND

Proverbs 23:7 — For as a man thinks in his heart so is he. "Eat and drink!" he says to you, but his heart is not with you.

MENTAL ILLNESS IS PART of societal conversation much more than in the past. People are more transparent about it now. However, for many people, there is still a negative evaluation connected to any type of emotional or mental condition. Many visualize the extreme and violent behaviors depicted on television and movie dramas of sociopaths and assume everyone with a mental health condition fits the caricature.

Mental disorders refer to a wide range of conditions affecting your mood, thinking, and behaviors.

The Bible has a lot to say about the mind and its impact on our mood, way of thinking, and behaviors. We are told we are what we think about. We understand this to mean the thoughts we dwell on determine who we become. Keep your heart (mind) with diligence because the issues of life spring from it. Because of this, Paul tells us to meditate on things that are true, noble, pure, lovely, of good report, virtuous, and praiseworthy. This is immediately after admonishing the believer to be anxious for nothing and trust God so his peace can guard our minds. Mental illness is a spiritual attack on the thoughts by the enemy that takes root and alters mood, ways of thinking, and behavior. God has the power to win the battle with Satan over the minds of his people, but it starts with us surrendering our minds to Him.

Write a personal reflection about your beloved so you can be specific when you intercede on his behalf. You can take pieces of the example as appropriate and add different aspects that apply to him.

(**Example**) He has struggled with depression and has a family history of disabling mental illness. It has been a barrier in his relationships with his wife, family, and friends. He withdraws socially and does not engage consistently and effectively with those who love him and whom he loves. Depression is a thief stealing his joy, peace, potential, and life.

Reflection on your beloved:

On Day 23, let us pray (as applicable) that:

1. He will recognize and acknowledge his mental illness.

2. God will reveal Himself to him as the healer of all illnesses.

3. God will reveal to your loved one how his thoughts are destroying his mental health.

4. He will have a moment of clarity when God can shine light and peace into his mind.

5. He will read Philippians 4:8 and see it as the antidote to his poisonous thought life.

6. He will begin intentionally meditating on empowering things and rejecting depressing and anxiety-producing thoughts.

7. He will be open to a counselor about his mental illness.

Add any additional prayer requests for him.

›————————————————————————————————————‹

›————————————————————————————————————‹

›————————————————————————————————————‹

›————————————————————————————————————‹

Reflection on your prayer and fasting time:

›————————————————————————————————————‹

›————————————————————————————————————‹

›————————————————————————————————————‹

›————————————————————————————————————‹

God's revelation to you today:

›————————————————————————————————————‹

›————————————————————————————————————‹

›————————————————————————————————————‹

›————————————————————————————————————‹

Praise and Thanksgiving:

›————————————————————————————————————‹

›————————————————————————————————————‹

›————————————————————————————————————‹

›————————————————————————————————————‹

As he thinks in his heart

so is he.
Proverbs 23:7

Day 24

The Power of Compassion

1 Peter 3:8, 9 — Finally, all of you be of one mind, having compassion for one another; love as brothers, be tenderhearted, be courteous; not returning evil for evil or reviling for reviling, but on the contrary blessing, knowing that you were called to this, that you may inherit a blessing.

IN A WORLD STEEPED in sin, the evil people do to one another can be so loud we miss the quiet acts of compassion done one-on-one, person-to-person, in all corners of the earth. Compassion is sympathetic pity and concern for the sufferings or misfortunes of another. And though it seems compassion is decreasing while indifference is increasing, we can see that even among the godless, compassion is still esteemed. Often, though, compassion is directed to strangers in greater amounts than to those with whom we share a roof, meals, and bloodlines.

This should not be so.

Compassion is a fully biblical directive, and it is to be made available to everyone we encounter, whether strangers, family, or friends. And though many are unbelievers, it is only from the influence of God that they can act in compassion toward another. For Christians, this should be one of the chief traits of character flowing through us from connection with the Holy Spirit.

True godly compassion goes beyond a feeling of sympathy and moves to actions. We bear one another's burdens. We take the load off another when we see them unable to carry it further, or even before, so they aren't worn down. We intervene when there is a need we can supply. We give when we can give, and we help when we can help.

And we do so even when it requires us to sacrifice ourselves, our comfort, our time, our money, our whatever.

Write a personal reflection about your beloved so you can be specific when you intercede on his behalf. You can take pieces of the example as appropriate and add different aspects that apply to him.

(**Example**) He lacks compassion at times because he cannot see beyond himself, his moods, thoughts, and wants. His self-centered thoughts stunted his emotional maturity and made it almost impossible for him to see the needs of others, including his wife, or sacrifice himself to help.

Reflection on your beloved:

On Day 24, let us pray (as applicable) that:

1. God will remove the spirit of self-pity and self-centeredness from him.

2. God will develop in him a heart of compassion and other-centeredness.

3. God will convict him when he ignores or overlooks his family's needs.

4. He will demonstrate compassion in an active, specific way toward others motivated by the Holy Spirit movement in his mind and his heart.

Add any additional prayer requests for him.

Reflection on your prayer and fasting time:

God's revelation to you today:

Praise and Thanksgiving:

Be of one mind having

compassion for others.

1 Peter 3:8, 9

Day 25

LIVING ON PURPOSE

Mark 1:38—But He said to them, "Let us go into the next towns, that I may preach there also because for this purpose I have come forth."

PURPOSE IS A WORD that is overused and probably misused in the current culture. In previous generations, people often just lived day to day, as many still do, and never asked, discovered, or sought their purpose. They grew up, secured a job, went to college, married, had children, worked, paid bills, lived, and died. Now, especially in the Western culture, many are seeking or pursuing their purpose. This, in and of itself, is not a bad thing.

Purpose, as described by the world, though lofty, often remains in the realm of the temporal and it centers on the individual at its core.

God made us for a purpose. Even Jesus had a specific purpose. He only did things to advance His purpose. For all who follow Christ, we have the mission of being His witnesses to a lost world. However, individually God has given us all purpose which directs the way we fulfill the mission He has given to the church. And He gives us gifts or develops gifts in us to allow us to be excellent in doing the thing(s) He created us to do.

When we walk in His way and follow His counsel, we have joy, enthusiasm, and fulfillment in our lives.

Write a personal reflection about your beloved so you can be specific when you intercede on his behalf. You can take pieces of the example as appropriate and add different aspects that apply to him.

(**Example**) He doesn't know he has a purpose. Gifts he may not recognize come from God and have the potential to impact this world. But he has focused on having a job, being a business owner, and achieving worldly success, rather than fulfilling his purpose. Purpose doesn't happen immediately. It requires vision, intensity, and commitment even in the low times. The world is poorer for the want of him doing what he was created to do. He is poorer for not living in the purpose God intends for him.

Reflection on your beloved:

_____

_____

_____

_____

On Day 25, let us pray (as applicable) that:

1. God will kindle in him a desire for purpose in his life.

2. God will send godly men into his life to help him find direction.

3. God will make clear to him what his purpose is by giving him joy, enthusiasm, and fulfillment when he does that thing.

4. He will recognize purpose is about eternal things more than temporal.

5. He will follow God's leading and step out in faith to pursue his purpose.

6. God will give him a spirit of excellence in any role He places him.

Add any additional prayer requests for him.

>————————————————————————————————<

>————————————————————————————————<

>————————————————————————————————<

>————————————————————————————————<

Reflection on your prayer and fasting time:

>————————————————————————————————<

>————————————————————————————————<

>————————————————————————————————<

>————————————————————————————————<

God's revelation to you today:

>————————————————————————————————<

>————————————————————————————————<

>————————————————————————————————<

>————————————————————————————————<

Praise and Thanksgiving:

>————————————————————————————————<

>————————————————————————————————<

>————————————————————————————————<

>————————————————————————————————<

For this purpose

I have come forth.

Mark 1:38

Day 26

WISDOM IS THE PRINCIPAL THING

Proverbs 8:11 — For wisdom is better than rubies, and all the things one may desire cannot be compared with her.

THE WORLD DEFINES WISDOM as a combination of knowledge, experience, and good judgment. The wise person employs those traits in making decisions. Wisdom is a trait often relegated to the old, and old at heart, after many years of messing things up and then learning from their mistakes. When you say the word, it conjures a picture of a quiet, peaceful white-haired, robed individual who makes great tea and tweetable statements leading people to great depths of understanding, which changes their lives. But the picture created by movie producers of our day reflects nothing of the true source, accessibility, and availability of wisdom.

In this paradigm, wisdom is optional; when needed we can glean from another to use situationally, but there is no condemnation for the unwise.

The Bible has a different definition and application for wisdom. From a biblical perspective, wisdom is not optional, for the alternative is existing as a fool. The Bible personifies wisdom as the Divine. There is no benign other who can counteract the lack of wisdom in God's view. It is wisdom or foolishness. Wise or foolish. God or the enemy. Nothing else.

The wise person is more than just someone who makes prudent decisions. The Bible says the wise acknowledge God IS, and He is their source. The wise listen and follow the counsel of others, love wisdom and understanding, are pure, peaceable, gentle, willing to yield, full of mercy and good fruits, not partial, and not hypocritical. The picture is quite different from the tea-drinking, robed sage of the movies.

A fool is far more than just a poor decision-maker. He is lost because he lives as though God doesn't.

Write a personal reflection about your beloved so you can be specific when you intercede on his behalf. You can take pieces of the example as appropriate and add different aspects that apply to him.

(**Example**) He is a smart person; knowledgeable, experienced, and yet foolish. He knows a lot about God but doesn't know Him as his source. He ignores or doesn't follow through on the good counsel of others and is unwilling to assess his behavior, thinking, and choices to determine why things aren't going how he thinks they should in his life. He lacks many of the characteristics inherent in the wise.

Reflection on your beloved:

On Day 26, let us pray (as applicable) that:

1. God will open his eyes to see where he is acting foolishly.

2. He will acknowledge his foolishness.

3. He will recognize all wisdom is from God, and he will ask God for it.

4. He will follow wise counsel in all areas of his life instead of his ideas.

5. God will transform his character to become pure, peaceable, gentle, willing to yield, full of mercy and good fruits, not partial and not hypocritical.

Add any additional prayer requests for him.

_____

_____

_____

_____

Reflection on your prayer and fasting time:

_____

_____

_____

_____

God's revelation to you today:

_____

_____

_____

_____

Praise and Thanksgiving:

_____

_____

_____

_____

For wisdom is

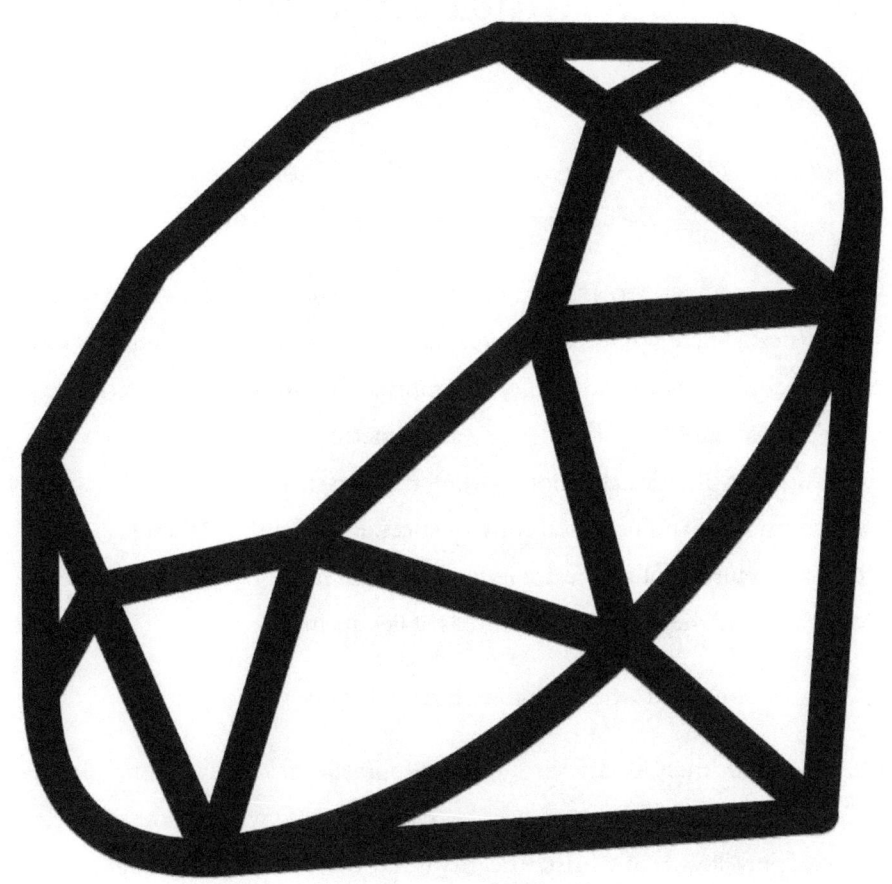

better than rubies

Proverbs 8:11

Day 27

LIVING WITHOUT COMPROMISE

Proverbs 11:3 — The integrity of the upright will guide them, but the perversity of the unfaithful will destroy them.

INTEGRITY IS BEING HONEST and having strong moral principles and moral uprightness. There was a time when a handshake between businessmen was enough to secure the word and fidelity of a contract between them. Integrity was common practice and lack of integrity was shameful. Today the world has embraced the idea of situational ethics allowing them to surrender ethical behavior to the circumstances and potential consequences. Many of the highest leaders in the world are examples of a decrease in integrity. It is not shocking to fact-check politicians and find they have told hundreds of lies during their years of "service."

Integrity is relational and when it is absent, relationships suffer.

The Bible is clear integrity is a virtue, not circumstantial or situational. Jesus spoke His Word and fulfilled it in every aspect of His life without the slightest deterrence. For followers of Christ, integrity is more than just honesty and moral principles. It is obeying God consistently in all things, even when it is hard. It is doing to others only what you would have them do to you. It is being consistent in your word, even when it is not to your advantage.

Facing the ultimate sacrifice of eternal separation from His Father and the Holy Spirit, Jesus kept His covenant to save a dying world.

Write a personal reflection about your beloved so you can be specific when you intercede on his behalf. You can take pieces of the example as appropriate and add different aspects that apply to him.

(**Example**) He does not walk with integrity. He makes promises in relationships he does not always keep. He expects from others what he does not give in return. He makes decisions based on what feels good rather than what is right. He defends himself as right when all evidence shows a different truth. He doesn't admit to being wrong without ascribing blame to another.

Reflection on your beloved:

﹥━━━﹤

﹥━━━﹤

﹥━━━﹤

﹥━━━﹤

On Day 27, let us pray (as applicable) that:

1. God will convict him of his lack of integrity with himself.

2. God will convict him of his lack of integrity in his marriage.

3. God will convict him of his lack of integrity in other relationships.

4. He will admit this deficit in his character and surrender to the pain of change.

5. He will recognize how relational breaches come from his broken promises.

6. He will be faithful to his commitments even when he doesn't feel like it.

Add any additional prayer requests for him.

———————————————————————————————

———————————————————————————————

———————————————————————————————

———————————————————————————————

Reflection on your prayer and fasting time:

———————————————————————————————

———————————————————————————————

———————————————————————————————

———————————————————————————————

God's revelation to you today:

———————————————————————————————

———————————————————————————————

———————————————————————————————

———————————————————————————————

Praise and Thanksgiving:

———————————————————————————————

———————————————————————————————

———————————————————————————————

———————————————————————————————

The integrity of the

upright will guide them

Proverbs 11:3

Day 28

BOLD STEPS TOWARD COURAGE

Ezra 10:4 — Arise, for this matter is your responsibility. We also are with you. Be of good courage and do it.

C OURAGE FROM A BASIC definition is the ability to do something you fear or to demonstrate strength in a difficult time. The world applauds courage. Random stories of ordinary people risking life and limb to save a stranger melt our hearts and restore, momentarily, our faith in people. When people face difficult times or circumstances or grief, thrive instead of falling under the weight; we call this courage. Courage can be defined in many ways, but its manifestation is in action. We see it and then we declare someone has it.

Yet courage is so much more.

The world has an accurate but incomplete understanding of courage. God's Word fills in those gaps in its usual counterintuitive manner. We say, "Have courage" and yet I couldn't find one instance in the Bible where this is the directive. In the biblical paradigm, courage is not something you "have" it is something you "are." "Be of good courage," and "Be strong and of good courage" are the directives given to God's people throughout the Bible. Courage then becomes not something you display in a moment because of a specific threat or during a period because of a particular struggle.

Courage is part of your "being" that happens when you are walking with God.

This courage not only allows you to face your Goliath, but it also requires you to confess your Bathsheba. Courage allows you to celebrate your Jericho but compels you to acknowledge your Ais. It allows you to conquer your wilderness but permits you to agonize in your Gethsemane. Biblical courage is not about demonstrating strength, it is about embracing weakness, knowing that only in recognizing our weakness is His strength made perfect through us.

I can "be" because He "Is."

Write a personal reflection about your beloved so you can be specific when you intercede on his behalf. You can take pieces of the example as appropriate and add different aspects that apply to him.

(**Example**) He has courage, but he isn't courage. He will face any danger to protect his family but won't face his pain so he can protect them from generational trauma. He will stand up for his family but won't stand up to his family. He dares to conquer, but not to surrender. He doesn't dare to face his sins, weaknesses, and fears because he thinks those behaviors represent who he is and he can't reveal that part of himself and still be loved.

Reflection on your beloved:

On Day 28, let us pray (as applicable) that:

1. God will show him that he can be truly known and loved.

2. God will give him an understanding of courage.

3. God will give him the courage to face his sin, weakness, and fears and conquer them.

4. God will give him the courage to stand up for himself.

5. He will learn how to wait on God.

6. He will surrender to God in everything.

Add any additional prayer requests for him.

_____

_____

_____

Reflection on your prayer and fasting time:

_____

_____

_____

God's revelation to you today:

_____

_____

_____

Praise and Thanksgiving:

_____

_____

_____

Be of good courage

and do it.

Ezra 10:4

Day 29

THE ART OF CONNECTION

Proverbs 18:21 — Death and life are in the power of the tongue, and those who love it will eat its fruit.

EVERYONE KNOWS COMMUNICATION IS a critical part of maintaining loving, nurturing, and happy relationships. However, many people struggle with sharing at all. They talk but don't connect. We have all had failures in this area that created conflict in a relationship. We have all probably had conversations that created intimacy in a relationship. Yet, many avoid those open, consistent, and direct disclosures.

The reasons are as varied as the people. Some stay closed because they don't want to show their weaknesses, failures, or shortcomings. Others stay closed because they came from families who shared nothing, and they have not broken away from the mindset. Still others think no one cares about what they have to say, so they keep the minor and major things bottled up inside.

Yet, relationships, marriages, and partnerships fail because of the absence of true, open, vulnerable, and consistent communication.

In John 1, the Bible reveals another name of Jesus as the Word. Creation, except for man, came through the Word. Throughout the Bible, God is a communicator, consistently trying to draw us back to Him. He could have forced us with His power, commanded us with His sovereignty, or manipulated us with His knowledge. But He spoke. And He still speaks because He wants us to know Him and love Him for who He is. How we understand who God is and draw closer to Him is through talking and listening to Him. As people are made in His image, the way we understand each other and draw closer is the same as with God. Husbands are to love their wives the way God loves them. This should include telling their wives how they feel and what they think.

Those conversations should be life-giving.

Write a personal reflection about your beloved so you can be specific when you intercede on his behalf. You can take pieces of the example as appropriate and add different aspects that apply to him.

(**Example**) He does not share things or communicate well. He considers asking questions as being invasive. Sharing his feelings is challenging for him since it was uncommon in the environment in which he was raised. This causes a break in the connection with many of his important relationships.

Reflection on your beloved:

On Day 29, let us pray (as applicable) that:

1. God will teach him how to love.

2. God will convict him on the necessity and importance of communication.

3. God will teach your loved one how to have open, consistent, vulnerable, and life-giving communication with those who love him.

4. He will include others in his life by sharing the major and minor things.

5. He will listen openly and attentively when others are sharing with him.

6. He will show he cares, misses, and is interested in other people through his communication.

Add any additional prayer requests for him.

Reflection on your prayer and fasting time:

God's revelation to you today:

Praise and Thanksgiving:

Death and life are in the

power of the tongue.
Proverbs 18:21

Day 30

SACRIFICE OF KINDNESS

Ephesians 4:32 — And be kind to one another, tenderhearted forgiving one another, even as God in Christ forgave you.

KINDNESS IS NECESSARY, BUT not always available. It is intentional, thoughtful, and directional. Yet if you are kind, particularly if you are a man, many people see weakness. Some men are afraid someone will take advantage of them. However, when kindness is absent it breaks hearts, people, relationships, and communities. It is not an overstatement to say in the presence of kindness, many, if not most, of the world's problems would be solved. Because kindness in its essence, requires the sacrifice of self for the benefit of another.

Abuse, violence, sexual perversion, greed, neglect, and even poverty could be significantly reduced or even eliminated were kindness a foundational characteristic of all.

The Bible is not quiet on kindness. It is not a milquetoast quality dismissed by God as unimportant. It is a fruit of the Spirit, a character trait of God, and of those who claim His name. Paul tells the church to be kind to one another, but not just to those within the church, but to all. Kindness requires us to go out of our way or step out of our comfort zone.

God has sacrificed and done exponentially more for us and He commands it of us for others.

Write a personal reflection about your beloved so you can be specific when you intercede on his behalf. You can take pieces of the example as appropriate and add different aspects that apply to him.

(**Example**) He is not a kind person anymore like he used to be. Unless it is a crisis when he feels needed, he doesn't show appreciation, demonstrate politeness, or act like he cares at all. The simple courtesies are natural when you are being intentional, thoughtful, and directional are missing from his interactions and he has become mean and hurtful.

Reflection on your beloved:

>————————————————————————————————<

>————————————————————————————————<

>————————————————————————————————<

>————————————————————————————————<

On Day 30, let us pray (as applicable) that:

1. God will convict him of his unkind attitude and behavior.

2. He will acknowledge he is often mean-spirited and will desire to change.

3. God will heal his mind from whatever is triggering his unkind attitude and behavior.

4. He will perform an act of kindness this week for you.

5. He will become intentional and thoughtful toward you.

6. He will become intentional and thoughtful toward others he has been unkind to.

7. God will rebuild relationships that were broken because of his unkindness.

Add any additional prayer requests for him.

>————————————————————————————<

>————————————————————————————<

>————————————————————————————<

>————————————————————————————<

Reflection on your prayer and fasting time:

>————————————————————————————<

>————————————————————————————<

>————————————————————————————<

>————————————————————————————<

God's revelation to you today:

>————————————————————————————<

>————————————————————————————<

>————————————————————————————<

>————————————————————————————<

Praise and Thanksgiving:

>————————————————————————————<

>————————————————————————————<

>————————————————————————————<

>————————————————————————————<

And be ye kind

one to another

Ephesians 4:32

Day 31

LIFE BY DESIGN

John 10:10 — The thief does not come except to steal, and to kill, and to destroy. I have come that they may have life and that they may have it more abundantly.

THERE ARE POCKETS OF society, small but significant groups, coming out of the hypnotic trance of materialism and recognizing they are miserable because they have wasted years making a living, but they have no life. Troubled marriages, disconnected children, surface friendships, and wasted health are the collateral damage from chasing the delusive American dream. Because of this, believers and non-believers alike, are teaching people how to "actualize," reach their potential, contribute to making the world better, and have a life. Much good is being taught, learned, and implemented by these individuals. Millions of people are attracted to this new way of thinking and are changing their lives for the better.

Many of them are missing the crucial part, however.

Our Father, who is in heaven, sent His Son in the person of Jesus to give us the total package. Throughout His time on this earth, Jesus repeatedly promised life to His followers. It was easy for Him to do because He is Life personified. Anything we define as good excluding Jesus will never bring us life. There is no life without Christ. Period.

Seek Him. When we seek Him, He promises to add all these other things we have been chasing after. And what is super cool is when God gives you something, no one can take it from you except Him.

That's real security.

The Bible says where your treasure is, there will your heart be also. Why the heart? Because the heart is life. When the heart stops, death happens. When our focus is on the stuff and the stuff disappears, so does life. But when our heart is centered on Christ, life is continuous and abundant.

Write a personal reflection about your beloved so you can be specific when you intercede on his behalf. You can take pieces of the example as appropriate and add different aspects that apply to him.

(**Example**) He is living, but he does not have a life.

Reflection on your beloved:

_____

_____

_____

On Day 31, this final day of the intercession, let us pray (as applicable) that:

1. God will reveal Himself to your loved one as the source of Life.

2. He will fully and completely surrender his life to Christ, His Savior.

3. God will embrace him in His love, and he will have an experience, not just an understanding of Him.

4. God will give him a life beyond his imagination and then bless him with other things.

5. He will begin living a life that fulfills the potential God placed in him.

6. He will prioritize his existence in a life-giving order: God, wife, children, ministry/purpose, family, friends, work, etc.

Add any additional prayer requests for him.

_____

_____

_____

Reflection on your prayer and fasting time:

_____

_____

_____

God's revelation to you today:

_____

_____

_____

Praise and Thanksgiving:

_____

_____

_____

I have come that they

may have life abundantly.

John 10:10

Congratulations

CONGRATULATIONS ON COMPLETING THIRTY-ONE days of fasting and prayer for your divinely assigned prayer focus and honoring your commitment to *Pray It Forward* on his behalf.

I know God has done something amazing in you. I don't have any doubts. I pray and have been praying your prayers have transformed your loved one.

Just like you, I want it to happen immediately. However, as we said at the beginning, some miracles happen over time.

While you wait, we encourage you to worship. God's timing is perfect, even when we don't understand it.

Don't put this off until another time or when things are better. Go straight into these days of focused praise from the days of focused prayer.

For the next thirty-one days, we will praise and worship the God of perfect love, wisdom, and timing.

I have chosen thirty-one psalms and thirty-one of my favorite praise and worship songs to bless you and keep you focused on the trustworthiness and faithfulness of God and not your current circumstances.

David tells us to praise God with timbrel and dance; to praise Him with stringed instruments and organs AND praise is still very individual.

I don't believe David is prescribing a structure of praise but rather describing an attitude of praise.

If you imagine singing, instruments, and dancing on any occasion, you will likely associate joy and enthusiasm with the event. Most people would willingly attend such an occasion and not have to be forced. This is how we should come with our praise to God.

As we begin these next thirty-one days of praise, you can approach it differently.

- Praise verbally for each theme we prayed for in the first thirty-one days.

- You can use the scripture for each day as the focus on your praise for the day by reading it throughout the day or memorizing it.

- You can use the song of the day as a starting point and then choose a scripture that speaks to the characteristics of God highlighted in the song.

- Or you can allow the Holy Spirit to direct you to what you need to know about praise based on what He knows you need.

Praise is to God, but it is also personal. There is no one right way to do it. You can be vocal and expressive, or quiet and reflective. If He is the point, He will receive it.

We want to praise Him for who He has been throughout the thirty-one days of intercession and for who He will be in the next thirty-one days. The next thirty-one days will draw you so much closer to God and will change your perspective on how you see life, the one divinely assigned to you and yourself.

Turn the page and let's get started.

Praise Break #1

Psalm 34:1 — I will bless the Lord at all times; his praise shall continually be in my mouth.

DAVID WROTE THIS PSALM during his time in the wilderness running from Saul, who was trying to kill him. God anointed him as the next king, but years later, he was not yet on the throne. Instead, there was a hit on his life from the current king, his father-in-law. He was so anxious and exhausted that he committed an act that resulted in the priest and his family being slaughtered.

With all going on in his life, he turns his heart and mind to God and declares that his blessing and praise of God will be continuous even in the bad times. David starts many of his psalms with complaints and ends with praise.

The challenge of praising in the difficult times, in the waiting season, is not new. Throughout the Bible, we see God's people struggling during the down times. But God is faithful. He has not changed. And so now, while you wait for God to work in your loved one, commit to worshiping when previously you would have complained. Recognize God for all He is and all He is doing, even what you can't see. And don't stop serving Him while you wait for the answer to your intercession.

On Day 1, you prayed for God to illuminate his heart, as he had long been surrounded by the darkness of this world. Today, celebrate and give thanks to God for several profound truths.

First, He is the embodiment of Light, capable of dispelling darkness wherever it resides, simply through His divine presence.

Second, He is the living Word, and as your beloved opens the door to his heart, Christ will find a dwelling place within.

Third, He radiates beauty and has the power to transform all things into their most beautiful form in His perfect timing. Last, God is love, exemplifying vulnerability, surrender, intimacy, and humility in His unwavering commitment to reconcile us with Him.

Additional praise:

>————————————————————————————————————<

>————————————————————————————————————<

>————————————————————————————————————<

>————————————————————————————————————<

Thank God for the light you already see in your beloved:

>————————————————————————————————————<

>————————————————————————————————————<

>————————————————————————————————————<

>————————————————————————————————————<

Praise Song: **John Waller, "While I'm Waiting"**

From everlasting to everlasting

You are God.

Psalm 90:2

Praise Break #2

Psalm 90:2 — Before the mountains were brought forth, or ever You had formed the earth and the world, even from everlasting to everlasting, You are God.

THE TEACHING THAT GOD was, is, and will always be is accepted in the Christian world because the Bible says it. We obviously can't prove it. We certainly cannot grasp it on any significant level with the capacity of our human understanding. It is a complete act of faith to believe God is everlasting. Yet we believe because we recognize for Him to be a God worth serving, obeying, or praising, He must be bigger than us. He must be different.

But we don't recognize how this truth impacts us and our need for Him.

In John 8:58, Jesus said to the Jewish leaders, "Before Abraham was, I AM". It is His "I AMness" that makes the void we all experience absent from Him impossible to fill. The God-sized void we all have is because He was filling space before we even existed. When we came to be, it was not just through Him from a creative perspective, it was in relationship to Him. Before our parents even knew us, He did. As He knit our parts together, He left space just for Him. He could have created us to automatically love Him, but He created us with the freedom to choose to love Him.

On Day 2, you prayed for God to guide your chosen one in acknowledging the God-sized void within him and initiating a transformative relationship with the divine. Today, praise God for being the perfect match for every individual, regardless of our unique differences. Rejoice it is by divine design he carries this void, serving as a reminder of his inherent need for God's presence and love. God, in His infinite grace, is ready to fill him with the profound and everlasting love He has always held for him. Praise God's work within your loved one to bring about wholeness, mending the fragments of the soul and spirit.

Additional praise:

>——<

>——<

>——<

>——<

Thank God for any time you have seen your beloved leaning toward God:

>——<

>——<

>——<

>——<

Praise Song: **Chris Tomlin, "Holy Forever"**

I will bless the Lord

at all times.

Psalm 34:1

Praise Break #3

Psalm 9:2 — I will be glad and rejoice in You; I will sing praise to Your name, O Most High.

MOST OF THE THINGS in this world that bring us happiness are temporary. When good things happen, it feels like the feeling will never end, and we will never forget it. But too often, if we look back a year, months, or sometimes even weeks later, we barely remember the details and we certainly are not still basking in the feeling of the moment.

Joy, as described in the Bible, is different. We can have joy even in sorrow. The source is Jesus in our lives. It doesn't mean bad times don't come. It doesn't even mean we don't feel sad or even depressed. But when we turn our attention to the fact we have Jesus, He has promised to never leave us, and we can trust Him, our joy sustains us, even when the circumstances are hard.

On Day 3, you prayed for your beloved to experience joy, knowing this joy would manifest through an encounter with Jesus. Today offer praise and thanksgiving for the truth in the divine presence of God, there exists an abundance of joy that knows no bounds. God, both willing and able, desires him not just to catch a fleeting glimpse of His goodness, but to bask permanently in the joy He bestows. Praise Him for being the ultimate source of joy, and your loved one will find this profound joy in Him alone, not in any earthly pursuit. Be confident even as we offer our praise, God is actively working to connect him to the source of true joy. Rejoice! He is preparing him to serve as a living testament to God's transformative power, impacting the lives of his family and friends who will witness his remarkable transformation.

Additional praise:

_____

_____

_____

_____

Thank God for any joy you have seen in your beloved:

_____

_____

_____

_____

Praise Song: **CeCe Winans, "I've Got Joy"**

I will be glad and

rejoice in You;

Psalm 9:2

Praise Break #4

Psalm 9:1 — I will praise You, O Lord, with my whole heart; I will tell of all Your marvelous works.

DAVID WAS VERY FAMILIAR with God and His marvelous works. But remember all the times when he complained about what God was doing? Throughout the psalms we read about David's unhappiness with his circumstances, blaming God for his troubles and asking how long it is going to last. And yet, he always returns to praise. Why?

God is marvelous. He is beautiful. He is love. We don't always remember to look at the beauty of His character when we are assessing the works of His hand or the things He allows. That is human nature. But in this journey of life and sanctification, it is not about how you start, it's about how you finish. You may have started with anger, complaints, and hopelessness when you were interceding for your beloved, but you can end with praise from your whole heart knowing He is marvelous because He is working for the good of you and your loved one.

On Day 4, you prayed for your beloved to wholeheartedly embrace a relationship with Jesus Christ. Today, spend time in praise, celebrating the following revelations: God possesses a character of unparalleled beauty that will naturally draw your loved one to Him in due course. He stands as the Water of Life, providing nourishment to all who acknowledge their spiritual thirst. As the ultimate source of rest and freedom, He offers him the solace and liberation he seeks. Above all, God is love. His works are marvelous, testifying to His beauty and grace.

Additional praise:

_____

_____

_____

_____

Thank God for any joy you have seen in your beloved:

_____

_____

_____

_____

Praise Song: **Austin Stone, "How Marvelous"**

I will tell of all

Your marvelous works.

Psalm 9:1

Praise Break #5

Psalm 100:4 — Enter into His gates with Thanksgiving, and into His courts with praise. Be thankful to Him, and bless His name.

READING AND PONDERING THIS verse we discover our first posture should be gratitude. No matter the circumstance, you always have something for which to thank God. If you begin to list it, there will be no end. Recognizing literally every good thing you have, from a place to sleep to organs functioning daily to sustain life, you cannot live without God. Even those who don't acknowledge Him breathe the breath of His grace every moment. Start everything with gratitude.

You are focusing on praise in these thirty-one days because it is harder for most people to praise in difficult times. Once you get into the gate, you can use praise to get to the throne. In the courts is where the throne is, where our Father sits, and waits for us to get close to Him. It is where you tell Him how much you love and appreciate Him since He spends so much time declaring His love for you.

Imagine a child curling up on her dad's lap rubbing his cheek, telling him that he is the best daddy ever. This describes you and God when you praise.

On Day 5, you prayed for your beloved to recognize all the things he has for which to be grateful. Today let's praise God. He has generously bestowed upon your loved one many reasons for gratitude. He is ready to transform his mindset, helping him appreciate all he possesses. God is an intimately caring presence in our lives, desiring closeness with us. He stands as a loving and benevolent Father.

Most importantly, He is ready to unveil His goodness to your beloved, opening his eyes to the abundance of blessings surrounding him.

Additional praise:

$>$———————————————————$<$

$>$———————————————————$<$

$>$———————————————————$<$

$>$———————————————————$<$

Thank God for any spirit of gratitude you have witnessed in your beloved.

$>$———————————————————$<$

$>$———————————————————$<$

$>$———————————————————$<$

$>$———————————————————$<$

Praise Song: **Brandon Lake, "Gratitude"**

Enter His courts

with praise.

Psalm 100:4

Praise Break #6

Psalm 25:4, 5 — Show me Your ways, O Lord; teach me Your paths. Lead me in Your truth and teach me, for You are the God of my salvation; on You I wait all day.

OFTEN WHEN WE PRAY, it is not to seek God's ways or be taught by Him, it is to declare our ways and express our will. David had a better understanding of the purpose of prayer than many of us do. This scripture can help us redirect our energy and get all our prayers answered. What a novel idea.

The maker is the one who knows best how a thing should be used. Ask Him. Praise God you have the privilege of going to the Maker of your beloved and asking Him to show you what path to take. Praise God when He shows you the truth about Himself and teaches you how to know Him better. Rejoice during the wait, even though it is hard. Give glory to God because He is the truth, you can trust Him in every situation and circumstance.

On Day 6, you prayed for the one entrusted to you to initiate seeking God in prayer. Today let's praise God because He encourages us to talk with Him about all aspects of our lives. He is ever attentive and never too preoccupied to listen to our prayers. As a prayer-answering Father, He remains steadfast in His commitment to respond to our needs. He desires your loved one's approach so He can impart divine wisdom and guidance. God will inspire him to join you in prayer, seeking guidance from Him. Ultimately, He will provide the direction and intervention necessary to meet his needs.

Additional praise:

Thank God for any time your beloved has prayed for God's guidance.

Praise Song: **CeCe Winans, "He's Not on His Knees Yet"**

Lead me in Your truth

and teach me.

Psalm 25:4, 5

Praise Break #7

Psalm 117:2 — For His merciful kindness is great toward us, and the truth of the Lord endures forever. Praise the Lord!

G OD IS NOT JUST great because He is God, nor because He says it in His Word. He is great and worthy of being praised because of His merciful kindness and His truth. God's kindness is different. It combines mercy. His kindness causes Him to mitigate the punishment or consequences we deserve for our wrongs because of His love for us. Of course, sin cannot be excused, so Jesus took our punishment so mercy and justice can co-exist. And Jesus, our Sin-Bearer, is the Truth that will endure forever.

Praise the Lord for His merciful kindness. What a gift of love to His children. When you consider all the mercy the Lord has given to you, it puts into perspective even the wrongs others have done to you. Praise Him. His truth endures forever. When God tells you the truth and sets you free you have a reason to praise. Praise Him. He is the Truth and foundation of your life even in the middle of chaos. Praise Him. He is the One you can hold on to and be free.

On Day 7, you prayed for your beloved to experience liberation through the internalization of truth. Today let's offer praise to God for the following affirmations: His truth stands unwavering and unchanging. He is ready to demonstrate to your loved one His Word is trustworthy and reliable. God has graciously provided the truth that holds the power to transform him. In a world where conflicting truths can entangle and restrict people; He represents the Truth offering genuine freedom. His truth extends beyond mere rules and boundaries; it provides guidance and purpose. Most importantly, His truth possesses the ability to infiltrate and liberate the self-imposed prisons of the mind, offering a pathway to emancipation.

Additional praise:

_____

_____

_____

_____

Thank God for any small way your beloved applies God's truth.

_____

_____

_____

_____

Praise Song: **Leanna Crawford, "Truth I'm Standing On"**

His merciful kindness

is great toward us.

Psalm 103:2-4

Praise Break #8

Psalm 103:2-4 — Bless the Lord, O my soul, and forget not all His benefits: Who forgives all your iniquities, Who heals all your diseases, Who redeems your life from destruction, Who crowns you with lovingkindness and tender mercies,

To BLESS IS SYNONYMOUS with praise in the Bible. David gives us more insight on when and why God should be praised. We get to be the silent observer to him working through his journey of praise. He reminds himself there are many benefits to serving and being in a relationship with the Lord. He is a forgiver, a healer, and a redeemer. He showers His children with lovingkindness and tender mercy. Why should we not praise Him?

Praise Him for all His benefits. This is the point of these thirty-one days of praise. Praise God now for being a forgiver of your iniquities. You prayed for thirty-one days about your loved one's issues, but I am sure there was a conviction about your deficits in some of those areas. Praise God for conviction and a clean slate. Praise God for healing diseases of the body, mind, and spirit. Praise God for redemption, knowing if not for His intervention in your life, your destination would be destruction. Praise God for His lovingkindness and tender mercy.

On Day 8, you prayed for healing for your beloved's mind and body. Today let's extend our praise to God, acknowledging His magnificent attributes: He is the Great Physician, possessing the power to heal. With a heart full of compassion, He is both willing and able to mend your loved one, tending to the needs of body and soul. He not only serves as a Healer but also a Comforter, providing solace during the challenging healing process. God is ready to mend both broken bodies and broken hearts, bringing restoration to every aspect of his being. Furthermore, as He heals, He can alleviate the pain of past wounds and hurts, offering a soothing balm to the afflicted soul.

Additional praise:

>————————————————————————————————————<

>————————————————————————————————————<

>————————————————————————————————————<

>————————————————————————————————————<

Thank God for any steps your beloved takes toward the healing process.

>————————————————————————————————————<

>————————————————————————————————————<

>————————————————————————————————————<

>————————————————————————————————————<

Praise Song: **Katy Nichole, "In Jesus Name (God of Possible)"**

He forgives your sins,

He heals your diseases.

Psalm 117:2

Praise Break #9

Psalm 148:14 — And He has exalted the horn of His people, the praise of all His saints—Of the children of Israel, a people near to Him. Praise the Lord!

W HAT DOES IT MEAN to exalt the horn of His people? What is a horn? Is this referring to a musical instrument? In this context, probably not, although that is one meaning. In this case, a figurative interpretation of horn should be used, which is power. But what power do God's people have He would recognize, let alone exalt? It is their praise. Praise to God is our superpower because it activates His power. The more we praise, the more might is activated for our good. Of course, we don't praise God to motivate Him to do things for us. We praise because He is worthy. However, the power is ours to access when we praise.

Praise God for using His strength to bless you. It is just one of the many ways He has demonstrated the value He places on you. Praise Him because your value was great because He designed you. Give glory to Him because He paid the ultimate price to redeem and restore you. Praise Him for your incalculable value based on Him. Rejoice because your worth doesn't have to rely on anything you do, say, or create. He has made Himself accessible to the ones He created so celebrate.

On Day 9, you prayed for your divine assignment to realize his God-worth, as we have called it. Today give praise to God because He is the ultimate source of worth, infusing each soul with inherent value. Recognize and rejoice God has planted eternity within our beings, emphasizing the enduring significance of our existence. He treasures your loved one not for what he does, but for who he is, valuing him above any of his actions. Thank God for His commitment to teaching him the profound truth about his worth in God's eyes. Through His divine presence and revelation, He will unveil Himself to him, reinforcing the realization of his immeasurable value.

Additional praise:

―――――――――――――――――――――――――――――――――――――

―――――――――――――――――――――――――――――――――――――

―――――――――――――――――――――――――――――――――――――

―――――――――――――――――――――――――――――――――――――

Thank God for the ways your beloved has recognized his worth in God.

―――――――――――――――――――――――――――――――――――――

―――――――――――――――――――――――――――――――――――――

―――――――――――――――――――――――――――――――――――――

―――――――――――――――――――――――――――――――――――――

Praise Song: **Crowder, Dante Bowe ft. Maverick City Music, "God Really Loves Us"**

He exalts the horn of His people,

the praise of His saints.

Psalm 148:14

Praise Break #10

*Psalm 66:20 — Blessed be God, who has not turned away my prayer,
nor His mercy from me!*

GOD THAT HEARS EVERY one of our prayers. This is amazing in a way we can't fully process. But even more amazing is He hears everyone's prayers, all the time, every day...and He answers. God doesn't just hear the prayers of the Christian. He hears every person's prayer, even those who aren't praying to Him. And His mercy turns toward those who pray. The writer of this psalm was talking about His relationship with God. He wasn't intentionally writing a chapter in the Bible for the billions of people who have read it. Yet, we get the privilege of His reflections. We learn another reason God is worthy of our praise is He has not turned away from our prayers. He has mercy for us.

Praise God for hearing all thirty-one prayers you prayed for the one entrusted to you and all the hundreds you prayed before this focused intercession. Praise God even when you are wrong. He doesn't turn away from your prayers. Bless God His mercy extends to you every day. Rejoice that He never tires of drawing to us, helping us, or saving us. Praise God, He can hear us while still attending to the other billions of people in the world. Give glory to God for seeing you, even when you don't see yourself.

On Day 10, you prayed for your assignment to cultivate self-awareness and gain insight into his own identity. Today let's offer our praises to God, recognizing the truth of God's unwavering awareness of your beloved and unconditional love for him. Give thanks for His boundless mercy that remains ever-present in your loved one's life. God has generously provided time for him to recognize and acknowledge his need for Him. In his moments of weakness, God is strong. The true image of God is inherently attractive, drawing your loved one toward Him. Praise God, as He pledges to walk alongside him during times of hopelessness, offering comfort and encouragement along the way.

Additional praise:

>———————————————————————————<

>———————————————————————————<

>———————————————————————————<

>———————————————————————————<

Thank God for ways your beloved has begun to see himself more honestly.

>———————————————————————————<

>———————————————————————————<

>———————————————————————————<

>———————————————————————————<

Praise Song: **Casting Crowns, "Just Be Held"**

Blessed be God

Who always hears my prayer.
Psalm 66:20

Praise Break #11

Psalm 142:7 — Bring my soul out of prison, that I may praise Your name; the righteous shall surround me, for You shall deal bountifully with me.

WHEN HE WROTE THIS psalm, David was in bondage because he was in a cave running from Saul. He wanted to be free to live his life and do the things he was accustomed to doing. He wasn't rushing to be king. He just wanted to fight for Israel with Saul, hang with his friend Jonathan, and be with his family. He wasn't literally in a prison, but he was imprisoned. He prayed for a time when he would be free, praise God, and be surrounded by others who praise Him.

Praise is not limited to good circumstances. David understood this and he praised God all the time. Praise God for your freedom from the bondage you experienced before choosing to intercede for this soul entrusted to you. Praise God for being with you in the prison and not abandoning you there. Praise God for the other women who have prayed for the men in their lives and seen God work miracles. They are the righteous surrounding you and the cloud of witnesses testifying to God's goodness, even if you may not know each other yet. Praise God, He dealt bountifully with you while your soul was in prison.

On Day 11, you earnestly prayed for your beloved to find liberation from the shackles of anger and bitterness. Today we unite in praise to God for the work He is doing in response to your prayers. God is a relentless chain-breaker who destroys the bonds holding us captive. His divine conviction is at work, guiding your loved one to understand the detrimental effects of his anger on himself and his family. With grace, He is revealing the hidden recesses where anger and bitterness have taken root within him. Praise God that He is instilling a heartfelt desire in him to break free from the bondage of his anger, fostering a yearning for change. Thank God for His mercy that erases the painful memories perpetuating this bondage, ushering in healing and release. Praise God for being the unfailing source of peace your loved one can experience, offering solace and tranquility amid the turmoil of anger and bitterness.

Additional praise:

Thank God for the ways you see your beloved being freed from his anger.

Praise Song: **Chris Tomlin, "Amazing Grace (My Chains Are Gone)"**

Free my soul

that I may praise Your name.

Psalm 142:7

Praise Break #12

Psalm 139:14 — I will praise You, for I am fearfully and wonderfully made; marvelous are Your works, and that my soul knows very well.

THE ATHEISTS HAVE NO reason to praise because they don't believe in the Creator. Many of them are scientists who are replete with awe, amazement, and even reverence for the body, earth, and galaxy that evolved from "nothing." You hear them talk about the wonders of the human body we can see and how wonderfully we are designed, and yet they exclude the designer. The psalmist does not make this mistake. He recognizes we are indeed fearfully and wonderfully designed by God, who does marvelous works. He says even his soul knows God's works. For me, this is a rejection of the need to "prove" there is a God. No, he says, my soul knows I am designed.

Give glory to God for designing you uniquely and as an image of Him. He cares about your life, health, and wellness, and it was included in the price He paid for you. You are not just a spirit with a body to keep you in time and space. He dwells in your body when you invite Him in. Praise Him for being accessible to the ones He created. Rejoice because He lives in you, you have a life in Him. Praise Him because despite your poor choices, you are still fearfully and wonderfully made, and He can and will restore you.

On Day 12, you prayed for your beloved's physical health and overall well-being. Today offer praises, worship, and thankfulness to the Creator for being the ultimate sustainer of his health and vitality. He has uniquely and wonderfully shaped your loved one, so worship Him for His wonderful works. Praise God for choosing to make his body His sacred temple. Offer praise and thanksgiving for this divine relationship. He is moving even now to impress upon your loved one the importance of not neglecting his health. In His infinite love and care, God remains a central figure in his physical well-being. Worship Him as the guide of this health journey.

Additional praise:

_____

_____

_____

_____

Thank God for the ways your beloved's health has improved.

_____

_____

_____

_____

Praise Song: **Nicole C. Mullen, "My Redeemer Lives"**

I will praise You

for I am wonderfully made

Psalm 139:14

Praise Break #13

Psalm 71:3 — Be my strong refuge, to which I may resort continually; you have given the commandment to save me, for you are my rock and my fortress.

THE WRITER RECOGNIZES GOD. He hasn't changed. We praise His name now and forever because He will be the same forever. He can be counted on. His stated values are demonstrated by His behavior. He promised to never leave. Whenever we go to Him, He is there as the rock and fortress. God is the only one whose choices and behavior perfectly align with His values. It is how we know and trust Him to be faithful.

Praise God for being unchanging, even when your faith and emotions waver in the storm. He is the One you have gone to continually, even as a last resort, and He was always there. Praise Him for being constant in the ever-changing circumstances of your life. Praise Him for being your rock and fortress, particularly in this difficult season. Go to Him daily because He has promised to be there, and His words are unchanging. Rejoice that His commandments have saved you from decisions you would regret. Give praise that in your weakness, He is strong.

On Day 13, you prayed for your loved one to align his values and behavior, and so today, offer praise and thanksgiving to God for His unwavering faithfulness. Even when your loved one's values and behavior may waver, God remains steadfast and unchanging. Praise Him for His consistency. God's faithfulness endures even when he may falter in his faithfulness to Him; be thankful for His enduring love. God serves as a rock and fortress for him to lean on, providing strength and support. As the ultimate model of constancy, God sets the example for your beloved. His commitment to him is unending and enduring, and for this, He deserves your gratitude.

Additional praise:

_____

_____

_____

_____

Thank God for the ways you see your beloved re-aligning his values.

_____

_____

_____

_____

Praise Song: **Hannah Kerr, "Same God"**

You are my rock

and my fortress.

Psalm 71:3

Praise Break #14

Psalm 42:5 — Why are you cast down, O my soul? And why are you disquieted within me? Hope in God, for I shall yet praise Him for the help of His countenance.

THE BIBLE IS FULL of stories of heroes of faith who had unheroic moments or periods in their lives. They became frustrated, fearful, or unhappy about their circumstances. This is not unusual or unchristian, it is just human. The author was depressed and recognized it. He questioned his thoughts and sadness. Throughout the chapter, he recounts the bad times and then counters with the memories of God's rescue and salvation. Hope in God became his antidepressant.

This has been a journey for you. There have been many bad memories over the past months or years, but there have also been victories, blessings, and interventions from God. Praise God for being your hope when everything seemed hopeless. Praise God for showing up on time, even when you wanted Him to come earlier or later. Give glory to God for not condemning you when you were cast down, disquieted, or depressed. Rejoice in the Lord always as a counterpunch to the enemy's depressive words and thoughts coming against you. Remember the goodness of God in the challenging times so you can maintain your hope in Him and praise Him.

On Day 14, we earnestly prayed for your beloved to consider seeking counseling for his emotional well-being. Today, give God praise for His attributes and the hope He brings. He is the ultimate source of hope for the one you are interceding for, a beacon of light in times of need. God stands as his unwavering help, providing guidance and support. His track record of showing up for His children is undeniable; praise Him for His consistent presence. He genuinely cares about your loved one's mental and emotional health, and for this, give Him worship. God is not condemning, but a source of understanding and compassion. Above all, He is inherently good, demonstrating love and grace to all who seek Him.

Additional praise:

_____

_____

_____

_____

Thank God for the ways you see your beloved being more hopeful.

_____

_____

_____

_____

Praise Song: **Matthew West, "The God Who Stays"**

Hope in God,

I shall yet praise Him.

Psalm 42:5

Praise Break #15

Psalm 118:21 — I will praise You, for You have answered me,
and have become my salvation.

H AVE YOU EVER CALLED someone for assistance, and they didn't answer? You needed their help, and they either didn't hear, weren't available, or just ignored you. God is not like this. He always answers. He promises when we call, He will answer. Because salvation is so freely given, we often forget to praise God for the gift. He answered our prayer for forgiveness and salvation. We know this because He doesn't force salvation on us. We must come to Him. Of course, He is the one behind the scenes convicting us, loving us, and drawing us to Himself. But ultimately, we must make the choice. When we do, God immediately answers and saves and forgives us.

Praise God for answering when you called on Him the last 45 days. You prayed for many different issues and concerns. You interceded for your beloved, but for yourself as well. You needed help. You needed to be saved, and He has, He is, He will. Praise Him for saving you from sin. Praise Him for saving you from detrimental decisions, the enemy's attacks, giving up on your beloved, indecision, and all the things He has saved you from every day. Praise Him that He will continue to save you if you call on Him.

On Day 15, you prayed your beloved would understand the need for forgiveness from God for his sins. Today, let's praise God, recognizing His merciful and redemptive nature. He is the ultimate Savior, ready to rescue and redeem those who seek His forgiveness. As a gracious forgiver, God extends His mercy and grace to those who come before Him in humility. He is always ready to answer whenever anyone calls upon Him, an ever-present source of support and love. God's love for him remains steadfast, even if he has not yet repented, and you can be grateful for His unending love and patience. He allows us to see our shortcomings and sins, offering the cure and the path to salvation. Moreover, He will continue to draw your loved one lovingly toward Him, extending His grace and guidance as he journeys toward repentance and forgiveness.

Additional praise:

_____

_____

_____

_____

Thank God for the ways you see your beloved seeking God's face.

_____

_____

_____

_____

Praise Song: **Elevation Worship, "O Come to The Altar"**

I will praise You

You are my salvation.

Psalm 118:21

Praise Break #16

Psalm 32:1, 11 — Blessed is he whose transgression is forgiven,
whose sin is covered. Be glad in the Lord and rejoice, you righteous;
and shout for joy, all you upright in heart!

ALL OF US HAVE experienced the gnawing, conscience-prickling, feeling of unconfessed sin. David certainly understood this. And because we have all felt the guilt and shame of sin, we also know the feeling of being forgiven by a family member or friend we have wronged. There is relief, joy, and restoration of peace. David says it is a blessing to know our sin is forgiven and covered. Then we can be glad in the Lord and rejoice.

Praise God for His inherent goodness and infinite capacity to forgive. Praise God we know we are covered if we go to Him in sincerity. With this knowledge, we connect with His strength to seek forgiveness from others we may have sinned against. We can rejoice when we follow His process for reconciliation because not only do we receive forgiveness, but blessings follow. We find solace in knowing, through His forgiveness, we are sheltered, our transgressions wiped away, and our souls renewed. Rejoice as you have been interceding for God's son, He has shown you areas you need to confess and has given you the blessing of freedom from those sins. Praise God even when the storms of life are raging and the circumstances around are bad, He is still good.

On Day 16, you prayed your beloved would seek forgiveness from those he had wronged. Today, praise God, acknowledging the transformation He is going to bring about in him. He is a forgiving God, abundant in grace and mercy. His inherent goodness shines through in His willingness to pardon and reconcile. God does not harbor grudges; instead, He offers opportunities for renewal and healing. As you offer praise, He is actively at work in your loved one's heart, stirring a desire for forgiveness and reconciliation. God stands ready to pour out the blessings of forgiveness and reconciliation upon him, ushering in a season of healing and restoration.

Additional praise:

_____

_____

_____

_____

Thank God for any steps your beloved has taken toward repentance and reconciliation.

_____

_____

_____

_____

Praise Song: **Jonathan McReynolds, "God Is Good"**

Blessed is he

who is forgiven.

Psalm 32:1

Praise Break #17

Psalm 130:3 — If You, Lord, should mark iniquities O Lord who could stand?

WHEN WE REALIZE NONE of us could stand if God were to mark our iniquities, it becomes a humbling reminder of our imperfections. This awareness makes it even more important to extend forgiveness and erase the wrongs of others when they sin against us. We understand without showing mercy and forgiveness to those who wrong us, we may not receive God's gracious forgiveness ourselves. This divine forgiveness is not a blessing we can afford to overlook. However, forgiveness is not always easy for us to give, as it is a divine act requiring a heart willing to extend grace. Fortunately, God not only forgives us but also grants us the will and the strength to forgive others. He is the wellspring of everything we need in the cycle of reconciliation.

Praise God for being our source. He not only forgives your sins but also makes Himself available to guide and support you on your journey of faith. You can rejoice that He doesn't tally your wrongdoings or hold them against you. Instead, He takes on the roles of both Judge and Advocate, ensuring that when you sincerely repent, God erases your sins. He offers you the gift of reconciliation, restoring your relationship with Him and empowering you to extend the same gift to others. You can celebrate the boundless mercy and forgiveness God offers, recognizing it empowers you to forgive others. His presence in your life is all-encompassing, guiding you in the path of grace and restoration, making Him the ultimate source of strength and love in your journey of faith.

On Day 17, you prayed for your beloved to find the strength to forgive those who have hurt and wronged him. Today, let's praise God. He is everything your loved one needs in all circumstances, providing support, guidance, and love. As both the ultimate Judge and Advocate, God navigates the complexities of justice and forgiveness. He is the model of forgiveness, teaching your loved one to extend grace to those who have wronged him. Through your prayers and His divine work, the Savior is actively softening your beloved's heart, fostering forgiveness and healing even in the face of deep wounds. Furthermore, God's divine love has the power to mend seemingly irreconcilable relationships in your loved one's life, leading to the beautiful possibility of reconciliation.

Additional praise:

Thank God for the ways you see your beloved seeking reconciliation even in small ways.

Praise Song: **Jason Nelson, "I Am"**

If You mark sin

who could stand?

Psalm 130:3

Praise Break #18

Psalm 112:1 — Praise the Lord! Blessed is the man who fears the Lord, who delights greatly in His commandments.

I N A WORLD FILLED with distorted images of what defines a man and dictates his actions, the prevailing notion often revolves around traits like independence, control, and dominance. However, the Bible presents an alternative, counter-cultural view of a man—one who finds his true happiness in dependence on God and a delight in following His lead. This portrayal of masculinity is not rooted in fear in the sense of being afraid of God. Instead, it speaks of a profound reverence for Him and a genuine deference to His divine will. It's about willingly submitting to God's purpose and plan, recognizing He is the one who orders our steps.

Praise God some men live out this scripture. Rejoice that Christ is the ultimate example of humble masculinity, who, despite being fully divine, came to Earth in perfect submission to His Father's will. He provided a living embodiment of how a true man lives his life, one marked by selflessness, humility, and obedience. Praise God for the joy accompanying this submission to Him. There is no need to fear the path God leads you on or the commandments He entrusts to you. Experience true happiness by embracing this kind of submission, as it aligns you with His divine order and purpose. This will foster a sense of fulfillment and contentment in your life's journey. Rejoice you can trust Him with surrender.

On Day 18, you prayed for your beloved to develop a biblical understanding of manhood. Today, let's offer praise to God for His guiding presence and transformative work in his life. He is the ultimate model of manhood, exemplifying virtuous leadership. God's leadership is not toxic, setting a positive example for him to follow. Praise God that He is actively at work, fostering connections between your loved one and other godly men, and offering valuable support and guidance. Give thanks to God because you know when your loved one submits to God's plan, He will become his source of happiness, filling his life with purpose and contentment. Thank God, who works even now to shift your loved one's paradigm of manhood, instilling values of humility and compassion as he looks to the divine example set before him.

Additional praise:

_____

_____

_____

_____

Thank God for the ways your beloved is shifting to biblical masculinity.

_____

_____

_____

_____

Praise Song: **Babbie Mason, "Trust His Heart"**

Blessed is the man

who fears the Lord.

Psalm 112:1

Praise Break #19

Psalm 128:3, 4 — Your wife shall be like a fruitful vine in the very heart of your house, your children like olive plants all around your table. Behold, thus shall the man be blessed who fears the Lord.

MARRIAGE IS A VERY self-centered union from the world's perspective. But the Bible clarifies when a man understands marriage from a godly perspective, seeks God's face for direction, and walks in His ways, he will be happy and will have a happy wife, children, and a home. The whole family prospers when God is the leader and center of the home. God is love and thus, anytime we follow His example and revere His Word, we will reap the benefits of a relationship with Him.

Praise God that He is love and He is the creator and sustainer of marriage. Praise Him that He wants you to be happy. Rejoice that He has a plan for your home to be restored and restructured around His principles and purpose. God will make you fruitful in your home and life when you are walking in His will. Any children you have or will have will be productive. Your love and marriage are worth fighting for, so praise God for His love that hasn't and won't give up on you.

On Day 19, you prayed for the one divinely assigned to you to gain an understanding of covenant marriage and how to establish one. Today, let's praise God, recognizing the work He is accomplishing within him. God is love and the foundation of a covenant marriage. Praise God for being the creator and sustainer of marriage, ensuring its sacred and enduring nature. His keen interest lies in your loved one's happiness, and He seeks to make both him and his home abundant and fruitful. As you praise, God is actively positioning a godly mentor to guide him along this path. Beyond personal happiness, He has a grand kingdom purpose He intends to fulfill within him, and we eagerly await the fulfillment of His divine plan.

Additional praise:

Thank God for the ways your beloved is changing his picture of marriage.

Praise Song: **Warren Barfield, "Love Is Not A Fight"**

Your wife shall be

like a fruitful vine.

Psalm 128:3

Praise Break #20

Psalm 127:3 — Behold, children are a heritage from the Lord
the fruit of the womb is a reward.

C HILDREN ARE A GIFT, and inheritance, from the Lord. They belonged to Him first, and he gave them to you to take care of, nurture, teach, love, and return to Him. It is a solemn and awesome responsibility that should not be dismissed or devalued. Because they are a gift from God, they have intrinsic value and significance to Him. Parents' attitudes toward their children should reflect this value. Yet, many parents don't. They see children as fun to play with, or a nuisance to interrupt them from more important things. But they don't see them as children of God entrusted to them to raise for their good and His glory.

Praise God that He is the perfect Father to you. If you have children, rejoice God trusted you with His child to love, teach, and nurture. Praise God for the inheritance He has blessed you with. Pay attention to the seriousness and significance of the responsibility. Praise Him for teaching you what He wants you to teach them. Give praises to Him even when it is hard, He is with you. You are a steward of God's blessing, and you should praise Him for all the children in your life, biological or not.

On Day 20, we lifted our prayers for your beloved to gain a deeper understanding of his role as a father or stepfather. Praise God, the epitome of a Good Father, offering unconditional love and guidance. God is never an absentee Father, even when your beloved may not fully acknowledge Him. His care extends to the happiness and well-being of your loved one's children, so praise Him for His watchful eye. In His grace, God is actively working on your loved one, specifically in his role as a father. The Lord has a purpose and plan for his children, and your beloved is a part of His plan. Thank God that He will guide him to an understanding of how-to parent for the good of the children and for the glory of God, ensuring His wisdom guides their journey.

Additional praise:

>————————————————————————————————<

>————————————————————————————————<

>————————————————————————————————<

>————————————————————————————————<

Thank God for the ways you see your beloved is connecting to his children.

>————————————————————————————————<

>————————————————————————————————<

>————————————————————————————————<

>————————————————————————————————<

Praise Song: **Chris Tomlin, "Good Good Father"**

Children are a heritage

from the Lord.

Psalm 127:3

Praise Break #21

Psalm 1:1 — Blessed is the man who walks not in the counsel of the ungodly, nor stands in the path of sinners, nor sits in the seat of the scornful.

THE BOOK OF PRAISE starts by outlining what NOT to do and who NOT to choose as friends. Don't get counsel from ungodly people, those who reject the wisdom of God. Don't hang out with individuals who are living in sin or who mock the Word of God and His will. There is no happiness in surrounding yourself with those kinds of people and friends. However, the blessing comes with a commitment to God's Word and, by extension, people who have the same commitment. The chapter then highlights the specific blessings that will permeate the life of the one who delights in God's Word.

Praise God for your relationship with Him, and for understanding His Word. Praise God this time of intercession and praise is founded on scripture. Rejoice you know His law and remain connected to His truth. Relish in His power over any other tool or book of self-development. Praise God that He has an answer for every question you have and He is not withholding it from you. Give glory to God if you have family or friends who stand with you on the scripture and don't lead you in the path of the ungodly. Praise God that He has or will put friends in your life who are godly, holy, and reverent so your life, work, and heart will thrive.

On Day 21, you prayed for your beloved to form more productive friendships. Today, let's join in praising God for what He is accomplishing in his social connections. He is a friend who sticks closer than a brother, offering unwavering companionship and support. God is inherently relational and the ultimate source of true friendship. His divine Word serves as the foundation for truly impactful relationships, guiding your loved one's connections with others. The perspective granted by His law brings delight and discernment in forming friendships. His Word is fruitful, shaping his character and interactions. God is working to bring friends into your loved one's life who share a mutual joy in God's Word, fostering meaningful and productive relationships.

Additional praise:

_____

_____

_____

_____

Thank God for any godly men who have entered or reentered your beloved's life recently.

_____

_____

_____

_____

Praise Song: **Yolanda Adams (featuring Donnie McClurkin & Mary Mary), "Lift Him Up"**

Blessed is the man

who walks with the godly.

Psalm 1:1

Praise Break #22

Psalm 30:3, 4 — O Lord You brought my soul up from the grave; You have kept me alive, that I should not go down to the pit. Sing praise to the Lord, you saints of His, and give thanks at the remembrance of His holy name.

DAVID KNEW A LOT about being on the edge, in the pit, ready to die, and being rescued by God. As much as he was a man after God's heart, there were many moments when he was ready to go to the pit. Many times, he was in the pit. God saved him so he could change course. This is praiseworthy. David knew it and he wanted anyone who heard this psalm to know it, too. And he wanted that to be the catalyst for praise and thanksgiving.

Praise God when you were ready to give up and give in on your husband and marriage, God pulled you up from your pit. Praise Him for creating a place of hope and expectation. Sing praise to the Lord for all He has done for you and shown you in the past two months. You are His child, and He has kept you alive and kept your marriage alive when you were on the edge.

On Day 22, you prayed for your beloved to break free from addiction, if applicable. Today, let's express our hope and trust in God's power and His work in his life. Thank God, His grace will break through the fog of addiction, granting him the ability to make one reasoned, discerning, and wise decision this week, resisting the destructive behavior and initiating a new path of healing and growth. Praise God His love, far surpassing anything addiction can offer, will pierce his heart, providing the true fulfillment and contentment he seeks. He will experience a moment of clarity, one that exposes the emptiness of his spirit and redirects him towards

God, choosing a path of spiritual and emotional wholeness over addiction. Praise the Lord your loved one will allow God to take the reins and be the Lord in one significant decision of his life, setting the stage for transformation and recovery. As he learns to say "no" to the flesh and addiction, he will awaken with alertness, restfulness, vibrancy, and strength. And he will recognize the stark contrast to the sluggishness, fatigue, fogginess, and pain accompanying a "yes" to addiction. Thank God that He will proactively address his addictions through counseling and actively seek recovery, embracing the support and resources available for his journey towards healing and liberation from addiction.

Additional praise:

_____

_____

_____

_____

Thank God for the ways you see your beloved seeking God's face.

_____

_____

_____

_____

Praise Song: **Hillsong Worship, "O Praise The Name (Anàstasis)"**

You brought my soul

up from the grave.

Psalm 30:3

Praise Break #23

Psalm 30:11, 12 — You have turned for me my mourning into dancing; You have put off my sackcloth and clothed me with gladness, To the end that my glory may sing praise to You and not be silent, O Lord my God, I will give thanks to You forever.

DAVID'S PSALMS ARE SO honest and relevant, that we can read and connect with them thousands of years after he wrote them. We don't have to wonder what he is feeling. Here he expresses praise to God for turning his situation around. At a time when he was in mourning about his circumstances, God was working behind the scenes to make it right. He shifted his mind and healed from the depressed, mournful state he was in because of the trials he endured. But God came and turned the mourning into dancing and gladness. When he remembered God, he could not stop his praise and thanksgiving.

Praise God that He has been shifting your mind during this process of intercession. When you pray so intently for someone or something, it can feel heavier before it gets lighter because you are thinking about it all the time. During those times, it is easy to give up and believe it will never happen. Give glory to God you are here because you didn't give up. You prayed, fasted, praised, and gave thanks through all the emotional and mental turmoil. Rejoice in His mercy and grace in protecting your mind from giving in to the natural rather than holding on to the supernatural.

On Day 23, you prayed your beloved would recognize and acknowledge his mental illness. Today, let's lift our hearts in praise to God, acknowledging Him as the ultimate Healer of all diseases. In the mind's battlefield, His Truth stands as a powerful force, capable of dismantling the lies the enemy seeks to implant in his thoughts. As the Prince of Peace, God brings serenity to the storm within, and as the eternal Light, He illuminates the path to clarity and understanding. Gratefully, He provides pure, beautiful, true, and just things he can experience and meditate on, fostering a mindset of gratitude and hope. In this very moment, God is at work, prompting him to take the courageous step of seeking help for his mental illness. With faith as our guide, let's rejoice in the assurance he will recognize and acknowledge his struggle, setting the stage for a journey of healing guided by the Holy Spirit.

Additional praise:

_____

_____

_____

_____

Thank God for any positive or hopeful thoughts your beloved expresses.

_____

_____

_____

_____

Praise Song: **Brandon Lake, "Praise You Everywhere"**

You have turned for me

my mourning into dancing.

Psalm 30:11

Praise Break #24

*Psalm 145:8 — The Lord is gracious and full of compassion,
slow to anger and great in mercy.*

T HIS IS SUCH A clear and direct description of the God we have the privilege of knowing, serving, and being loved by. He is full of grace. This is not just for salvation from sin. It is for the daily journey of our walk with him. We need grace to wake up, to go to sleep, and for everything in between. He overflows with compassion, recognizes our humanity, and is concerned about suffering, big and small. He is with us throughout. He has every right to be angry at our disobedience and misdeeds, and yet He is slow to anger and respond with mercy. These are reasons to praise.

Praise Him, He has given you some of His compassion. If He didn't, you would have given up on this beloved a long time ago. You certainly would not be sacrificing to intercede for him now. Your Heavenly Father put him in your life. Don't despise it but rejoice because your heart is soft and you look like your Abba! Praise God for His grace in allowing you to see your faults in this process and thank Him for the mercy that is new every morning.

On Day 24, we prayed God would remove the spirit of self-pity and self-centeredness from your loved one. Today, let's praise God that He is a God of compassion and the model of other-centeredness for him. Rejoice that He is gracious with your beloved and grants him new mercies as He is moving on his heart. Thank God that He will give him a heart of compassion for others in his life as he has received from God. Bless the name of the Lord for any acts of compassion he demonstrates during this time specifically.

Additional praise:

>——<

>——<

>——<

>——<

Thank God for any acts of compassion your beloved has demonstrated.

>——<

>——<

>——<

>——<

Praise Song: **CeCe Winans, "His Strength Is Perfect"**

The Lord is gracious

and full of compassion.

Psalm 145:8

Praise Break #25

Psalm 138:8 — The Lord will perfect that which concerns me; Your mercy, O Lord, endures forever; do not forsake the works of Your hands.

GOD HAS A PLAN for us. And despite what it looks like now, His plan is perfect for you. He shows mercy for us because we regularly get off course, question the plan, wonder if there is a plan, or boldly rebel against it. And yet His mercy surpasses our mess-ups. He will not forsake the plan unless we do.

Praise God that He has a perfect purpose for you. It will not go perfectly, but it will glorify Him perfectly. Be thankful His mercy endures and will endure beyond your planned interruptions, rebellions, and doubts. Rejoice that He has not, will not, and cannot forsake you. Praise Him for your redirection to this prayer and praise.

On Day 25, we prayed for your beloved to have a desire for purpose. Today, let's praise God for creating your loved one for a purpose. Praise God for the godly, purpose-driven men God is sending to intersect your loved one. Rejoice although His purpose and plan are not easy, they will bring joy, enthusiasm, and fulfillment to his life. Three things he lacks now. Praise God the Father, Son and Holy Spirit live on purpose. Give glory to God for His excellence and that He infuses excellence in those who walk in His plan for them.

Additional praise:

_____

_____

_____

_____

Thank God for the times your beloved is seeking or acting on his purpose.

_____

_____

_____

_____

Praise Song: **Big Daddy Weave, "This Is What We Live For"**

The Lord will perfect

that which concerns me.

Psalm 138:8

Praise Break #26

Psalm 111:10 — The fear of the Lord is the beginning of wisdom; a good under-standing have all those who do His commandments. His praise endures forever.

MANY PEOPLE SEE GOD as someone to fear. Even Christians who have access to the complete canon of scripture can sometimes think of Him in this way. But can being afraid of God translate into wisdom? No, I don't believe it can. However, reverencing God can lead to wisdom. How? Because the one who knows God enough to reverence Him rather than be afraid of Him has surrendered to God as the Lord. This compels them to do all God says, receive all God has to give, and make decisions based on God's Word and commandments. All of this is wisdom in action. The one who does this will praise God forever.

Take a moment to lift your voice in praise to the Almighty for the incredible wisdom He has graciously bestowed upon you during these past 56 days. His guidance has been unwavering, revealing aspects of the one for whom you are fervently praying. Offer your heartfelt gratitude to God for the understanding He grants as you humbly walk with Him, realizing His path is far superior to any of your devising. Remember, when you align your steps with His, the privilege of praising Him becomes an eternal joy.

On Day 26, we prayed God would illuminate areas where your beloved might act unwisely. Today, let our praises lift to the heavens as we acknowledge God as the very embodiment of Wisdom. Those who welcome Him into their hearts receive the precious gift of divine wisdom. Lift your voice in gratitude, thanking God for His generous bestowal of this invaluable gift. Anticipate with joy the transformative power unfolding when he earnestly seeks godly wisdom. Praise the Almighty for being the ultimate model of Wisdom, revealing not just what it is but how it manifests in our lives.

Additional praise:

_____

_____

_____

_____

Thank God for any wise decision you see your beloved make.

_____

_____

_____

_____

Praise Song: **Casting Crowns, "God of All My Days"**

The fear of the Lord

is the beginning of wisdom.

Psalm 111:10

Praise Break #27

Psalm 33:4, 5 — For the word of the Lord is right, and all His work is done in truth. He loves righteousness and justice; the earth is full of the goodness of the Lord.

GOD'S WORD IS IMMUTABLE. It is a fancy biblical word meaning He cannot change. His character, will, and promises are unchanging because what He says is always correct, true, righteous, just, and good. He is without fail or any variation. We can trust Him without question or hesitation. He is a God Who cannot lie like men do. He is a God of integrity. Our faith rests easily in Him when we believe this.

Praise God for His immutability. Humans are quite the opposite. He has been good to you throughout this process because it is who He is not because you are deserving of it. He calls you worthy because He promised to do so when He saved you. Rejoice in the truth of having one relationship in which you can place all your faith without fear. Bless the name of the Lord, for He is righteous and just. He will always be righteous and just with you. It may feel differently, but because He is God who cannot lie, you can trust Him.

On Day 27, we prayed God would convict your beloved for his lack of integrity. Today let's praise God that He is full of integrity and a model for His children. Praise Him: He is faithful when everyone else fails. Bless His power to change your beloved into a man after His own heart. Thank God for the work the Holy Spirit is doing in him right now as you praise. Rejoice God will heal the relational breaches caused by the beloved's lack of integrity. Praise His holy name.

Additional praise:

›————————————————————————‹

›————————————————————————‹

›————————————————————————‹

›————————————————————————‹

Thank God for any shifts your beloved makes toward integrity.

›————————————————————————‹

›————————————————————————‹

›————————————————————————‹

›————————————————————————‹

Praise Song: **Yolanda Adams, "Let Us Worship Him"**

His word is right.

His work is done in truth.

Psalm 33:4, 5

Praise Break #28

Psalm 27:1 — The Lord is my light and my salvation; whom shall I fear? The Lord is the strength of my life of whom shall I be afraid?

DAVID WAS, FROM A worldly perspective, one of the most courageous men in the Bible. He was a warrior who took down Goliath when even the king was afraid to face him. He fought lions and bears and men with equal fearlessness. David knew his strength came from the Lord. This is why he had no fear. But also, light dispels fear. When you can see what is happening around you, then assessment of risk is easier. Any risk David imagined in darkness could be overcome by the Light.

Praise God that He is your Light, Salvation, and Strength as well. If you have made Him Lord of your life, then there is nothing to fear. Many giants have come after you during these past two months. And the truth is many more will come. There is always a battle when God's people pray. But you can give glory to God because prayer is the best way to fight the battles coming, so you are already in the right posture. Rejoice God fought your battles. Bless the name of the Lord for being your strength in your life.

On Day 28, we prayed for your beloved to have the right kind of courage. Today let's give praise that God is his Light, Salvation, and Strength. Praise God that He will show the beloved he has no reason to fear because he is loved. Give thanks to God because He won't change His feelings about your loved one despite the sins, weaknesses, and fears He already knows about. Rejoice for God is moving on his heart right now to make courageous decisions in work, family, health, finances, and spirit. Praise Him for being a God that He can safely surrender to.

Additional praise:

_____

_____

_____

_____

Thank God for the ways your beloved has shown courage recently.

_____

_____

_____

_____

Praise Song: **Selah, "You Are My Hiding Place"**

The Lord is my light

whom shall I fear

Psalm 27:1

Praise Break #29

Psalm 55:17 — Evening and morning and at noon I will pray, and cry aloud, and He shall hear my voice.

PRAYER CAN BE CONFUSING or seem out of reach for people when Christians make it seem lofty, high-minded, and exclusive. Prayer is talking to God like a friend. A friend who can do more than listen and empathize but can intervene. Anyone, anywhere, can talk to God and He will hear and answer. Anyone! David knew he could call on God at any time and in any emotional state, and he would be heard.

Praise God for hearing you when you talk. And just as important, you have experienced the truth God is communicating with you as well. He wants to have an ongoing conversation about everything in your heart and mind. Rejoice that He is not like the gods of the heathen who have ears, but don't hear, and have mouths but don't speak. God is the model communicator, so thank Him for setting the standard for you in all your relationships.

On Day 29, we prayed your beloved would understand the significance of communication in expressing love. Today let's exalt God, who embodies connection as the Word—the very source of genuine connection. He not only listens but also talks, and for this, we are grateful. Rejoice in the assurance God, Who is love, can impart this wisdom to the one for whom you are interceding. Let us offer praise for the Holy Spirit's conviction working within him, guiding, and instructing on the lessons of love, connection, and effective sharing. Praise be to God for His life-giving Word bringing transformation to your husband's life.

Additional praise:

_____

_____

_____

_____

Thank God for improving communication with your beloved.

_____

_____

_____

_____

Praise Song: **Vicki Yohe, "In the Presence Of Jehovah"**

I will pray all day

and He shall hear me.

Psalm 55:17

Praise Break #30

Psalm 117:2 — For His merciful kindness is great toward us, and the truth of the Lord endures forever. Praise the Lord.

GOD'S MERCIFUL KINDNESS IS great toward us! And yet it is often taken for granted, abused, or misunderstood. No characteristic of God is better than another simply because He is perfectly complete in all His ways. However, there are aspects of Him we don't experience every day because it is not warranted. We don't see miracles every day because we don't need miracles every day. However, His merciful kindness sustains our lives moment by moment. We could not survive our sins and the consequences thereof if not for his merciful kindness. The truth of who He is endures forever. And we should praise Him for His truth.

Praise God for His kindness toward you throughout this journey of prayer and praise. There have been many ups and downs, but He has sustained you. Rejoice that He is a God who cares about the day-to-day lives of His people. Many people serve gods they don't expect to be in a relationship with. They see them only as punishers or rewarders, depending on their behavior. It is transactional. God calls you into a relationship. Give glory to God that He is walking with you right now and His intentional kindness follows you through every hill and valley.

On Day 30, we prayed your beloved would stop being unkind. Today let's praise God that He is the source of kindness and He is moving on his heart right now. Praise Him: He continues to extend merciful kindness to the beloved while He continues to work on character. Rejoice because everything you desire your loved one to be, God IS. Our heavenly Father will transform your beloved. Praise the Lord for healing his hurts so kindness is an outcome.

Additional praise:

><--<

><--<

><--<

><--<

Thank God for the kindness you see in your beloved.

><--<

><--<

><--<

><--<

Praise Song: **Tauren Wells, "Hills and Valleys"**

His kindness is great

His truth endures forever.

Psalm 117:2

Praise Break #31

Psalm 36:9 — For with You is the fountain of life; in Your light we see light.

WE HAVE SATURATED OURSELVES in scripture for sixty-two days and in the songs of psalms for the last thirty-one days. And at the end, it all comes back to the truth that God is Light and Life. There is nothing outside of Him satisfying the need for Him. When we surrender to truth, then we will start making a life, not just a living.

Praise God that He is the answer to all the needs you have. He has provided for you through sixty-two days of sacrifice and surrender. Some things you thought you wouldn't survive because the weight of intercession is heavy. Bless God who understands the weight of intercession and took His yoke and put it on you and took yours and carried it. Give glory to God that He has restored life in you. Look back on Day 1 and see the miracle God did in you. Praise the Lord for making life with Him deeper and more intimate than you have ever experienced. Shout hallelujah to His name.

On Day 31, we prayed your beloved would start making a life rather than focusing on making a living. Today on our last day, let's give praise to God that He is the source of life and light. Praise God that He is in love with this man entrusted to your intercession, and He died rather than let him be lost without a hope of salvation. Give glory to God for the transformational experience your beloved will have with Jesus. Bless God for the life he already has planned for him as he surrenders. Thank you, God, neither you nor your beloved will ever be the same again in Jesus' name. Amen.

Additional praise:

_____

_____

_____

_____

Thank God for light and life in your beloved.

_____

_____

_____

_____

Praise Song: **Carrie Underwood (ft. Vince Gill), "How Great Thou Art"**

For with thee is life

in thy light we see light.

Psalm 36:9

You did it!

We have reached the end of this part of the journey. Prayer and praise never end, but our structured time together is complete. Tomorrow there will be nothing to "do," no devotional to read, scripture to learn, or topic to pray for the man the Holy Spirit entrusted to your intercession.

Now what? It may feel anticlimactic. Especially if you are not seeing the changes yet. I get it.

The discipline, the focus, and the structure become something you depend on.

When it's gone, it can feel like the rug was pulled out from under your feet. This is normal.

You will be tempted to stop because the book ended. But don't yield to the temptation. I am giving you a heads-up so you can prepare for what you will feel and make a different choice.

The book was the beginning, not the totality of your prayer and praise.

You have a routine now. Don't stop. Adapt a new routine around what you have learned.

It doesn't have to look the same way it has for the past sixty-two days. God will direct you on what it will be for you. But it needs to be something.

Keep praying and praising. Pray for other challenges coming up day to day. Pray for a decision he must make at work, a health concern, a book you want him to read, or a friend you want him to meet. Pray and praise about whatever is going on in your life today.

Go through it again for another man in your life. Even in the best circumstances, the men in your life will need your prayers.

Use the extra journal space in the back, write new praises, choose new songs, and learn new scriptures.

Just don't stop.

Whatever you do, don't stop. You can even start a group with the book and facilitate the *Pray It Forward* framework with other women in need of it.

I want you to stay a part of the *Pray It Forward* family and share your testimonies with us. This is not just a book for me.

It is a lifelong connection of women who believe "prayer is the key in the hands of faith that opens heaven's storehouse" (White, 1892, 94) and who have surrendered to the journey for a man they love.

Reach out to me at the contact information in the back of the book.

I have been praying with you and for you and will continue. Thank you for allowing me to be a part of your process.

God needs more women who are committed to fighting on their knees.

Thank you for being one of us.

Continue to *Pray It Forward*!

Lorraine

Prayer Scripture Index

Praise Scripture Index

Alphabetical Index of Topics

Playlist Index

1. John Waller, "While I'm Waiting"

2. Chris Tomlin, "Holy Forever"

3. CeCe Winans, "I've Got Joy"

4. Austin Stone, "How Marvelous"

5. Brandon Lake, "Gratitude"

6. CeCe Winans, "He's Not on His Knees Yet"

7. Leanna Crawford, "Truth I'm Standing On"

8. Katy Nichole, "In Jesus Name (God of Possible)"

9. Crowder, Dante Bowe ft. Maverick City Music, "God Really Loves Us"

10. Casting Crowns, "Just Be Held"

11. Chris Tomlin, "Amazing Grace (My Chains Are Gone)"

12. Nicole C. Mullen, "My Redeemer Lives"

13. Hannah Kerr, "Same God"

14. Matthew West, "The God Who Stays"

15. Elevation Worship, "O Come to The Altar"

16. Jonathan McReynolds, "God Is Good"

17. Jason Nelson, "I Am"

18. Babbie Y. Mason, "Trust His Heart"

19. Warren Barfield, "Love Is Not a Fight"

20. Chris Tomlin, "Good Good Father"

21. Yolanda Adams (featuring Donnie McClurkin & Mary Mary), "Lift Him Up"

22. Hillsong Worship, "O Praise the Name (Anàstasis)"

23. Brandon Lake, "Praise You Everywhere"

24. CeCe Winans, "His Strength Is Perfect"

25. Big Daddy Weave, "This Is What We Live For"

26. Casting Crowns, "God of All My Days"

27. Yolanda Adams, "Let Us Worship Him"

28. Selah, "You Are My Hiding Place"

29. Vicki Yohe, "In the Presence of Jehovah"

30. Tauren Wells, "Hills and Valleys"

31. Carrie Underwood (ft. Vince Gill), "How Great Thou Art"

Pray It Forward Playlist

Playlist Link:

https://www.youtube.com/playlist?list=PL_GUzlMsbeSBxDxFemKDPGMPL
FhgKd6yT

About the Author

Lorraine Edwards is an international speaker, life purpose coach, and the host of *Live, Love, & Marry Wizerr,* a YouTube program geared at helping single and married women make wiser decisions in their lives and relationships. While she was initially a reluctant speaker, she eventually embraced the gift God gave her to speak and present seminars on relationships to single individuals and married couples, a unique opportunity and privilege for a single woman. She has been sought out for her godly relationship advice since she was a teenager because she was a voracious reader of Christian books on courtship, marriage, parenting, and relationship issues. Married women have consulted with her during difficult times in their marriages and have applied the counsel and seen God change their hearts and, in time, their marriages.

Lorraine believes all truth comes from God. He can use anyone He chooses as a vessel for the truth. After God showed her through a parable, "You don't need to have the disease to know the cure", she stopped questioning the opportunities to speak to married couples because she knows God has used her in the past and will continue to use her to help Christian marriages despite her single status. She has received rave reviews from married couples who have attended her seminars despite their initial skepticism.

The Holy Spirit inspired her to start a speaking and coaching business targeting single women so she could help them start healthy, godly marriages by being healthy and connected to God first. Her goal was to help them embrace their singleness and the reality of God's purpose for them now; learn to walk in their purpose so they are fully who He created us to be; to prepare for the partner they desire so they choose from a place of wholeness and not brokenness. She believes an ounce of prevention is worth a pound of cure.

She combines her religious and spiritual foundation with an educational background. She has a BA in Psychology and a Master of Social Work degree from Virginia Commonwealth University (VCU). Lorraine worked full-time as the Area Social Services Manager for The Salvation Army in Richmond, Petersburg, and Hopewell, Virginia for eight years before she was called to ministry at the Longburn Adventist College in Palmerston North, New Zealand, where she served as an Assistant Dean in the Girls Boarding House in 2020.

Since returning to the States from New Zealand, she is enjoying her new role as Owner/Speaker/Author at *A SINGLE Mission*.

Contact Lorraine:
Lorraine@asinglemission.com
Asinglemission.com

www.ingramcontent.com/pod-product-compliance
Lightning Source LLC
Chambersburg PA
CBHW021714120626
46545CB00004B/1547